That's What the Old Ones Say:

Pre-Colonial Revelations of God

That's What the Old Ones Say:

Pre-Colonial Revelations of God

Chief Joseph RiverWind
Assisted by Laralyn RiverWind

Marble, NC USA
2014

First Edition 2014
Printed in Charleston, SC USA

Cover illustration © 2014 David Farley

Permission can be obtained for re-use of portions of material by writing to the address below. Some permission requests can be granted free of charge, others carry a fee.

Word Branch Publishing
PO Box 41
Marble, NC 28905

http://wordbranch.com
sales@wordbranch.com

Library of Congress Control Number: On file

ISBN-13: 978-0692299609
ISBN-10: 0692299602

Table of Contents

Introduction: The Story Begins

The small fire was crackling and radiating a small bit of warmth while the effervescent light it emitted danced on the battle-hardened face of PipeCarrier. The dancing flickers of light forced the shadows to retreat into the crags in his face making the wrinkles indistinguishable from the scars. PipeCarrier is of the Lakota Nation, an Oglala Sioux who comes from a long line of holy men and warriors. It was a rich heritage that any proud Native would be honored to carry.

PipeCarrier's long black hair was neatly braided as it hung down to the middle of his back. His hair framed his face and made his dark, almond shaped eyes the focus of his features which did not entirely give away what he had seen during his times of war. A bittersweet story of birth and death packaged in one humble human being. His journey began by being born in a sweat lodge when his mother, after giving birth to PipeCarrier's brother, went to lodge for her ceremonial purification. What she didn't know was that there was one more little warrior waiting to come out. Thus, his destiny began amidst a sacred ceremony, and he hoped it would end the same way.

He grew up learning the traditional ways of the Lakota people from his grandfather, Ghost Dance Boy, who survived the massacre at Wounded Knee. He survived because Ghost Dance Boy's mother used her own body as his shield while the U.S. Cavalry soldiers' bullets ripped mercilessly through her body. Ghost Dance Boy lived against insurmountable odds, through an epic massacre known to everyone familiar with their American history. His elders knew he had a special destiny; a special place amongst his people in their history yet to be made.

Ghost Dance Boy taught PipeCarrier the proper way of praying with the sacred pipe, sent him on his vision quests to learn what path Creator had for him, the traditional ceremonials songs and how to conduct the sacred ceremonies of his people. PipeCarrier listened to his grandpa, Ghost Dance Boy, tell the stories of his Lakota people. As he grew up under his grandfathers instructions he participated in the traditional ceremonies and kept these ancient ways guarded and alive in his heart and spirit. These cultural anchors helped him get through the rough times when he was deployed during Desert Storm and they helped him when he returned home.

During battle in Iraq, PipeCarrier was the only one to survive an ambush by enemy forces that left him distraught with survivor's guilt but was welcomed home with open arms to the sound of the drums, the women ululating, and the community singing all while being honored and thanked by his elders for walking the warrior path. He was a warrior, battle-tried and true.

I pondered these things as I sat by PipeCarrier at the fire, listening to the crickets sing their evening songs to The Creator. The natural rhythm of nature was all around us. There we were, two Native American warriors in the forest with a warming fire, singing old songs on our buffalo-hide hand drums and telling stories from long ago. We were creatures in our natural habitat, at ease in the dense woodland.

I remember my own grandfather highly encouraging me to join the military and learn all that I could about the modern warrior ways. It was part of our family history as Jaguar Warriors, so each generation has served from the ancient times as protectors of our people to modern day armed forces. It is our duty to our Creator, our family clan, our people, and to our country.

Holding steady at 90%, Native Americans have the highest volunteer ratio for military service compared to every other ethnic group in The United States of America. As indigenous people many of us feel a deep calling to the warrior path. We have an obligation to the land of our ancestors and to many Native Americans it is an honor to be trained as warriors with a lifelong commitment for being willing to fight for this country and our people (which has come to mean a broader sense than what it may have meant to us generations ago). We have participated in every conflict and war that this country has been in even though we weren't given the right to vote until 1942.

Native people continued to serve in the military even though we didn't have religious freedom on our own land until 1978. Despite the historical mistreatment we will continue to serve because this land will always be the land of our ancestors. Every mountain, river, valley, and stone carries a story of a long ago time.

While some may consider these stories "old wives" tales to First Nations people it is our history, our life lessons, our explanations for why things are or why things happened. The old stories have a broad range of topics including the times when tribes of red haired giants walked the land and the buffalo roamed free across the plains. When the star people fell from the heavens and took our women to the time when the Great Waters covered the earth. This includes the heartbreaking stories about the times when the fires will come and the earth, as well as mankind, will be devastated.

These were some of the things we sat around the fire talking about that cool spring evening after singing old medicine songs on our buffalo hide hand drums. PipeCarrier stoked the fire with a twig and then used it to light his canupa(sacred prayer pipe pronounced Cha-noo-pa).

"This fire is a good fire," PipeCarrier said with a peaceful smile as the firelight gleaming in his dark eyes danced like two candle flames in a room.

I nodded knowing what he meant when he said this. Native people chuckle about how other people build their fires. We see people build them taller than a man, and they burn white hot. Or some may build them so they suffocate themselves so that you have to keep blowing on them over and over. You see, a good fire is one that's built well enough to give off light and warmth while requiring minimal continued effort to stoke, but most importantly, small enough to look across the top of it and be able to hear the voice of the person who is sitting across from you. It is more intimate and personal when you share a fire as PipeCarrier and I were doing that evening.

I drifted off in deep thought about how Creator had brought me to this moment. As an infant, I was adopted and raised by my grandparents because of turbulent situations in the family at the time. When I was older I would visit my father who had become a pastor later on in his life. As a result, whenever I would go visit for the summer I would be in and out of the church, bouncing from one denomination to the next, but I never doubted the existence of God. Even so, when I left to join the Army at the eager age of seventeen, a seed of hatred toward the church was already angrily guarded in my heart. That seed was planted nice and deep in the fertile soil of my embittered heart.

The Church: The institution of bondage and death that supported historical genocide in the name of God. The religious organization supporting the total cultural destruction of tribes around the world with a heartbreaking and evil history against indigenous people. Specifically, the atrocities committed in the name of God against my tribe. The Taino grew more and more poignant in my consciousness. We, the Taino, were the ones who discovered Columbus wandering lost in the ocean. We were the first native people to be called Indian. The Native American Holocaust on this continent began with my people.

Understanding that this sounds harsh, but I am being completely honest with how I felt during those younger years in my life and how many Native people feel today. It was not a hard decision, therefore, to leave the church and return to a more traditional Native American spiritual path. I realized later that God had been graciously walking with me. I'm sure He occasionally just shook His head wondering when I was going to finally wisen up.

On my spiritual quest, I was honored to sit and listen, learn, and talk to elders from many First Nations tribes: Elders of the Comanche, Dineh (Navajo), Apache, Anishinabe, Aztec, Cherokee, Muscogee Creek, Cheyenne, Lakota, and Mohawk shared their stories with me. I listened eagerly to these stories that were passed down from generation to generation, honored to be gifted with the knowledge that cannot be bought or begged off someone.

They are stories that need to be told, need to be shared, need to be heard, need to be kept alive beyond the years of the storytellers. These are stories that were told before missionary contact, and I realized with each added story that I listened to had heard them before . . . not from my tribe but from another ancient tribe who has left an impacting legacy on the earth several of the greatest stories ever told within a book called the Bible. Stories of the flood and the Tower of Babel are examples of two biblical stories that can be heard among the First Nations stories.

I could not come to grips with these similarities for a long time. I could not even bring myself to admit the undeniable and obvious truth. Years had passed in my life and that well-guarded seed of hatred had put down strong roots of bitterness and produced its poisonous fruit of malice, prejudice, and scorn. The one thing I could not deny was there was a connection between our Native American people and God. He spoke to our ancestors in a way that we would understand Him. He had made himself known to us through the earth and the that there was a familiarity to them. In things of His creation, through messages in dreams, and prophecies, and visions given to the spiritual leaders.

Chapter I: Taino, the Tribe of First Contact

It is strange to me that when I answer the question, "What tribe are you?" that many people become extremely puzzled. Most have never heard of the Taino, yet we are the people of first contact. They know the name of the man who is reputed to have "discovered" us. Yet, unless they are a history buffs or well-read in Native American subjects, they do not know us.

By 1492, the territory of the Taino spanned from the island of Boriken (typically called Puerto Rico today) throughout the eastern Caribbean islands, Bimini (also known as Florida) and as far north as upper Georgia. There, the Muscogee Creek people called us "Toasi" which means "people of the Cassava Bread Griddle." Cassava bread is traditional bread that we make out of the yucca root and we cook it on the griddle called a "toa." We were master seafarers and traded with tribes throughout the southeast. Many words that we use in everyday English come from my Arawak Taino language. For example: Canoe (canoa), savannah (Sabana), tobacco (Tabacu), manatee (Manati), barbeque (Barbacoa), hammock (Hamaka), hurricane (Huracan),and many more.

I remember one night sitting in the car with my father up in the rainforest mountains of Boriken (Puerto Rico) where I was born. That area of the mountains is called "Las Indieras" which translates as "The Indian Lands." We were looking at the stars, and my dad said, "One day I will go back home, up there in the sky beyond the stars." His pensive brown face looked longingly into the evening sky. The Warrior constellation was above us which most people know as Orion. The sound of the coqui tree frog filled the cool rainforest mountain air and I looked to where he was pointing.

I was about twelve years old on that starry night and we had just left a church service where Creator had lifted the blinders from eyes of both my little brother and me. We had a vision – both amazing and terrifying. I needed to tell someone what happened… someone who would believe me. After that epic church service, I told my father what I had seen and I could tell that he completely believed me. He put me in the car and drove me up to the top of the mountain. From there, there was a clear view of the sky. Once we had parked he asked me to tell him again but to try to remember every detail as best as my memory would allow. I began to tell him what I had experienced at the church:

I sat in the not-so-terribly-comfortable front row pew next to my stepmother as she prayed. As my mind wandered, I looked back at everyone in the church praying, shouting, and making a big ruckus praising the Lord.

The music was really loud, and when I say really loud, I mean loud like only Caribbean people can make loud. My wife, Laralyn, says that my people only have one volume when we speak and that is "Taino volume." It is yet to be proven, but it is strongly hypothesized that my Taino people are incapable of what some cultures call a whisper. While microphones are rarely needed to augment a well-formed Taino mouth, they are always greatly appreciated at an event, making it much more fun. Try to imagine an ear-drum piercing, cranked up sound board, shrieking loud praise and worship music, then turn that up even more. The phrase "ear splitting" comes to mind.

We were sitting on the front pew, turned around looking at the scene behind us. When I spun back around toward the pulpit, all of a sudden I saw smoke start to billow from the pulpit! It began to roll down the steps leading up to the altar. It was pure white and silky, if smoke can be described as such. There was no scent but I felt a powerful presence in the room as I saw the smoke rolling closer toward me.

Even though I didn't smell the smoke, I knew fire only meant one thing, and it was serious. Everyone else being so distracted with eyes closed or dancing about, I realized they hadn't noticed the smoke at all. So at the top of my lungs, I yelled, "The church is on FIRE!"

"Halleluyah! Praise the Lord!" people in the congregation shouted as I kept yelling over and over again, "The church is on FIRE!" It seemed to me that the more I yelled, the more fervent people became in their praise and worship and the more I became frustrated. I grabbed my little brother by the arm and yelled over the shouting and praising "Come on, we have to get out of here!"

We ran down the middle of the church and out the double doors into the front parking area. We ran as far as the edge of the road and turned around to look back expecting to see people running out with flames jumping off their backs, accompanied by screams of agony. Instead, I stood there in utter shock at what I saw. On each corner of the church exterior were immense columns of pure white light nearly engulfing the entire building with their radiance-. Within each column, through the intensity of the light, I could just barely make out a figure standing there holding a sword of fire with both hands clasped around the hilt at chest level with the tip pointing down. I knew at once that these were angels. Not the typical winged, chubby baby angels you see drawn by most artists.

No, these were warrior angels. They were powerfully intense to look at and an experience that I will never forget.A glance back told me that the smoke was now pouring out through the middle doors of the church that remained open after our mad dash to safety. As I stood there in awe trying to catch my breath, everyone who was hanging out outside was looking at us standing there gawking at the church.

"Do you see them?" I asked the younger crowd of people who were outside. "Don't you see them? How can you not see them?" I yelled to anyone who would listen.

"Do you see them?" I asked my little brother. He nodded his head yes without taking his eyes of the angelic warriors standing guard at the church.

The coqui's (a tiny tree frog that is indigenous to the Caribbean rain forest) continued their nightly serenade of "kokee, kokee kokee" as the moon lazily drifted its way up into the cool evening sky. The temperature was brisk up in the mountains and a small breeze wove its way around us as I finished telling my dad about what I saw. We began to talk about many things that had to do with the Bible. He told me stories about supernatural experiences that had happened to him, to my grandfather and to other family members. He told me of family members who'd seen angels . . . and demons.

Then he slowly turned his attention back to the sky, and we sat in silence for a little while. This allowed me time to really think about what he was speaking before I answered. This is not unusual in our culture, and I have found that many people who are not raised in an indigenous culture can only stand the silence for a short amount of time. There always has to be noise of some sorts going on whether it's a TV or music. No wonder it is so difficult for people to connect and know the more intimate things about God. In American culture we have a hard time sitting still and knowing anything.

Psalm 46:10(KJV) *"Be still, and know that I am God:"* (YHVH -Stern, 1998)

Our elders teach us that Creator made us with two ears and one mouth, and we are to use them in that order. Listen more than we speak and think before we let our words come out of mouths. Being somewhere between a child and an elder, I am still trying to master this art and am far from achieving any level of mastery at it. But on that night, I sat there next to my dad, listening intently. I knew that I must remember this conversation between us and that many times I would look back upon this memory as a beautiful treasure.

My dad then looked at me, and he pointed to the vast sky full of brilliant stars. It looked even more beautiful from our view up in the mountains.

"You see all of those stars out there?" he asked me quietly. "Our people call the stars the campfires of the dead, those who have passed on to the spirit world. One day we will all go back home to the Creator. You have to be ready all the time because you never know when that day will come."

"Our Taino ancestors were always ready to be taken home to YaYa which is one of the names our people have for God and in the old stories. He had a son called YaEl whose symbol is a fish. It is interesting to note that YaEl in Hebrew means The Son of Yah. YaYa means The Supreme Spirit of Spirits," he continued. "They were given prophecies of things that were going to happen like the prophecy of the Talking Leaves."

John 4:24 *"God is spirit; and worshippers must worship Him spiritually and truly."* (YHVH -Stern, 1998)

"Our Taino people were also given prophecies about the things to come. There were ancient stories from our oral tradition that had been preserved with each generation. Our ancestors waited in great anticipation for these prophecies to become fulfilled." My dad paused and cocked his head to the side as if intently listening for something in the distance. After what seemed to be an eternity of silence he looked at me once again and said," Perhaps I will tell you some of that on this special day . . .."

Chapter II: Ancient Taino Indian Prophecy

"En el tiempo de las guacara, (In the time of the caves-ancient times) our Taino people were given prophecies of things to come that would change our world forever," my father said as he gazed longingly into the night sky.

The old ones foretold that three strange war canoes would come to our shores and that these war canoes would be filled with pale-faced, bearded men who were hicotea guami'ke'na (hee-ko-te-ah gua-me-ke-nee which translates to "covered like turtles." These hicotea Guami'ke'na would carry with them Talking Leaves which would bring further knowledge about Creator. With the advent of these Talking Leaves, there would come a great destruction of our people and way of life.

November 19th 1493 was a day that would forever change my Taino people's world. Never again would life be the same as it had been for centuries or millenia. As one, my people had arrived at a crossroad. Just as the old prophecies foretold, the three strange war canoes called La Nina, La Pinta, and La Santa Maria were sighted off the coast of the shore of Kiskeya. These strange "canoes" brought a message of eternal life with their cold steel swords standing by as if waiting for orders. The Bible came off those ships which we would soon recognize to be the Talking Leaves foretold. Unfortunately its advent came with a terrible price. (Rouse, 1992)

"Do you see?" my father sorrowfully asked me. "The Talking Leaves that were foretold reached our shores. The pages resembled leaves and even the paper is made from trees. What was amazing is that they contained a code (written language) that held the very words of Creator God. Our people flocked to the faith. But the witness that came with the Word was not what was expected."

~~~

Columbus is Discovered Lost at Sea

Christopher Columbus first lands in the Bahamas on 12 October 1492 in a three-ship expedition from Spain. Although he is given credit with the "discovery" of the Americas, Columbus merely sailed the same routes that other sailors had been aware of for generations. For example, the Icelandic Viking, Leif Ericson, is credited with the so called "discovery" of Newfoundland around 1003 and there are Cherokee stories that speak of the tribe of white men called "Welsh" who landed in present day Mobile, Alabama centuries before DeSoto came through their lands. (Deacon, 1966)

By 5 December 1492, Columbus arrived at western Kiskeya (Hispaniola-Dominican Republic), where he
~~~

founded the colony of La Navidad. Christopher Columbus described the Taino people in letters to Queen Isabella and King Ferdinand of Spain.

Columbus reports on his voyage to King Ferdinand and Queen Isabella of Spain:

These people in the Caribbean have no creed and they are not idolaters, but they are very gentle and do not know what it is to be wicked, or to kill others, or to steal...and they are sure that we come from Heaven....So your Highnesses should resolve to make them Believers, for I believe that if you begin, in a little while you will achieve the conversion of a great number of peoples to our holy faith, with the acquisition of great lordships and riches and all their inhabitants for Spain. For without doubt there is a very great amount of gold in these lands....

The people of this island [Hispaniola], and of all the others that I have found and seen, or not seen, all go naked, men and women, just as their mothers bring them forth; although some women cover a single place with the leaf of a plant, or a cotton something which they make for that purpose. They have no iron or steel, nor any weapons....They have no other weapons than the stems of reeds...on the end of which they fix little sharpened stakes. Even these they dare not use....they are incurably timid....

I have not found, nor had any information of monsters, except of an island which is here the second in the approach of the Indies, which is inhabited by a people whom, in all the islands, they regard as very ferocious, who eat human flesh....

They brought us parrots and balls of cotton and spears and many other things, which they exchanged for the glass beads and hawks' bells. They willingly traded everything they owned. They do not bear arms, and do not know them, for I showed them a sword, they took it by the edge and cut themselves out of ignorance. With fifty men we could subjugate them all and make them do whatever we want. (Columbus, 1493)

It is interesting to note Columbus' error in stating that we had no creed yet he also says that we believed they had come from heaven. One does not even understand the concept of heaven without some type of spiritual belief. Indeed, we did have spiritual beliefs. Apparently, at the time of this letter, our ancestors had not decided to divulge information about our spirituality to the newcomers.

Recorded Biblical history replays itself in the story of the Taino and that of King Ferdinand and Queen Isabella. A common biblical phrase is that there is nothing new under the sun. We can find the same spiritual cycle or pattern in the Taino narrative that was written down thousands of years ago further strengthening this eternal claim. My eyes were opened to this revelation from an Inuit elder that was formerly a Baptist preacher and is now a traveling bible teacher with a beautiful ministry sharing in-depth biblical truths. (Suuqiina, 2008)

We can examine this particular similarity by first looking in the books of 1 Kings and 2 Kings, we find the story of Queen Jezebel who was the daughter of Ethbaal, King of the Phoenicians and one of the wives of Ahab, King of the Northern Kingdom of Israel. She is described as being a worshiper of Ba'al and an enemy of God who ordered His prophets to be killed. She also encouraged her husband, King Ahab, to abandon the worship of the Creator in exchange for Ba'al and Ashtoreth. Jezebel's name translates into "Where is the Prince?" This was part of a ceremonial chant that was uttered when worshipping Baal during different times of year when he was considered to be in the underworld. Ceremonies for these false deities included ritualistic orgies as well as infant and child sacrifice by fire. (Hackett & Coogan, 2001)

In 1 King 21, we find the story of a man named Naboth. He was a humble man of God who owned a vineyard that had been passed down for generations in his family. Unfortunately for Naboth, it was inconveniently situated adjacent to the palace. King Ahab wanted to expand his garden so he sought to purchase the land. However, Naboth refused to sell the land which was the family inheritance. King Ahab pouted that he was not getting what he wanted, so Queen Jezebel fabricated evidence against Naboth for blasphemy and promptly had him stoned to death. Naboth's land was then confiscated for the evil king and queen.

Interestingly enough, an amazing parallel can be seen centuries later in Taino Indian history. The land and resources that were an inheritance to my Taino people for over two thousand years was suddenly coveted by one of the most powerful world leaders: Queen Isabella of Spain. Their scout, Columbus, had reported back to Spain that gold medallions were worn by the elite of our Taino society. Gold fever struck. The monarchy wanted gold-filled land at any cost. Nothing and nobody would stand in the way of Spain getting it. Lives would be lost and it did not matter to the Spanish monarchy the price innocent lives to get it.

In the Biblical story of Naboth the queen's name is Jezebel. However, it is important to note that the letter "J" is new to the English language, having been invented roughly 600 years ago. Its origins typically lie with an "I" or "Y." Jezebel is the Anglicized transliteration of the Hebrew word אִיזֶבֶל ('Izevel/'Izavel) which is ironically the same name as the Latinized name Isabella, bride to King Ferdinand of Spain.

Ecclesiastes 1:*9 "What has been is what will be, what has been done is what will be done, and there is nothing new under the sun." (YHVH -Stern, 1998)*

Solomon was right when he wrote this. What was done to the Hebrew man Naboth so many centuries ago was being perpetrated on a larger scale with my people. A dictator with an overactive sense of entitlement was willing to shed blood to take the land she wanted.

The atrocities committed at the hands of the conquistadors against my peaceful people were horrific. Hanging people 13 at time representing Jesus and the 12 Disciples was common as well as sadistic torture and murder. The following engravings depict what the Spanish Conquistadors did to my ancestors. These are graphic images for their time and just as emotionally impacting today.

"They would cut an Indian's hands and leave them dangling by a shred of skin for not gathering enough gold ... [and] they would test their swords and their manly strength on captured Indians and place bets on the slicing off of heads or cutting of bodies in half with one blow.(Casas, 1552)

"They built a long gibbet, low enough for the toes to touch the ground and prevent strangling, and hanged thirteen [natives] at a time in honor of Christ Our Savior and the twelve Apostles. ...Then, straw was wrapped around their torn bodies and they were burned alive." (Casas, 1552)

"[The Spaniards] took babies from their mothers' breasts, grabbing them by the feet and smashing their heads against rocks. .."As the Spaniards went with their war dogs hunting down Indian men and women, it happened that a sick Indian woman who could not escape from the dogs, sought to avoid being torn apart by them, in this fashion: she took a cord and tied her year-old child to her leg, and then she hanged herself from a beam. But the dogs came and tore the child apart; before the creature expired, however, a friar baptized it." (Casas, 1552)

"Because he did not give the great quantity of gold asked for, they burned him and a number of other nobles and caciques (Chiefs)... with the intention of leaving no prince or chieftain alive in the entire country." (Casas, 1552)

"They threw into those holes all the Indians they could capture of every age and kind. ... Pregnant and confined women, children, old men [were] left stuck on the stakes, until the pits were filled. ... The rest they killed with lances and daggers and threw them to their war dogs who tore them up and devoured them." (Casas, 1552)

Situations became so dire and the Taino people so desperate, that often parents poisoned their children and then jumped to their own deaths off the high cliffs into the ocean rather than face the worse fate of falling into the hands of the ruthless conquistadors. Much like the Israelites at Masada with the Roman Empire encamped around them my ancestors saw death as being more preferable to living a life of slavery torture, and brutal abuse.

I will not go into all of the details of every evil that my ancestors endured. The accounts are gruesome and heartlessly cruel. By 1511, my people had been decimated which caused the remaining survivors to join forces and rebel against the conquistadors. Chief Hatuey, from the island of Caobana (Cuba), was the first chief to rise up against the Spanish and lead a rebellion. He is still celebrated today as Cuba's first national hero. His words are immortalized by a priest named Bartelomeas De Las Casas who later became known as "The Defender of the Indians." The young priest wrote several letters to King Ferdinand informing him of the ongoing genocide, pleading for the Taino to be freed, and imploring the king to bring the cruelty to end, decrying their actions as unchristian. In one of his letters, De Las Casas recounted the last words Chief Hatuey made to his Taino people before he was burned alive at the stake.

"Here is the God the Spaniards worship. For these they fight and kill; for these they persecute us and that is why we have to throw them into the sea... They tell us, these tyrants, that they adore a God of peace and equality, and yet they usurp our land and make us their slaves. They speak to us of an immortal soul and of their eternal rewards and punishments, and yet they rob our belongings, seduce our women, violate our daughters. Incapable of matching us in valor, these cowards cover themselves with iron that our weapons cannot break..." (Casas, 1552)

Before Chief Hatuey's execution, a priest asked him if he would accept Jesus as his personal savior so he could go to heaven. De Las Casas recorded Chief Hatuey's reaction and last words:

[Hatuey], thinking a little, asked the religious man if Spaniards went to heaven. The religious man answered yes... The chief then said without further thought that he did not want to go there but to hell so as not to be where they were and where he would not see such cruel people. This is the name and honor that God and our faith have earned. (Casas, 1552)

The witness of the Bible that was brought by the conquistadors made my Taino ancestors step back and reassess what they were experiencing. Could these people really have been the ones that were spoken of in the sacred prophesies? With every cruel and evil act committed in the name of God to my Taino ancestors, they said to themselves, surely this is not the God that we have always known. Now if get "saved" are we going to become like them?

Unfortunately, this is the legacy and impact the Bible has left on the indigenous people of this land. These heartless actions planted the seed of hatred in the hearts of the people's DNA. That seed put down a strong root of bitterness that has sapped the lifeblood of every First Nations person throughout the centuries. Regardless of whether or not they knew what happened specifically to my Taino people, every tribe from Alaska to South America has had their own "Trail of Tears." And so often God and the sanctioned concept of conquest in the name of God was used as the excuse for what was done to the First Nations people.

It is common for native people to only remember the horrors but there were many who were outraged and protested the treatment of the First Nations people at the hands of the Europeans. It began with two voices crying out for indigenous justice in the 16th century. These two men set the precedent for many Christians to follow throughout the history of First Nations people and the slow, painful, physical and emotional death that often has been a part of native life since 1492. Although these two men were passionate about their convictions their voices fell on deaf ears, but it is still there – echoing in the endlessness of our pain and reverberating in the hollowness of our loss. Before De Las Casas, Antonio de Montesino denounced the treatment of the Taino at the hands of the conquistadors on the island of Kiskeya (Dominican Republic). On the 21st of December, 1511, the fourth Sunday of Advent, Montesino's preached a fiery sermon to the Spaniards criticizing the colonial system, and decrying the abuse of the Taíno Indian people.

In his sermon, he enumerated the injustices being committed by the colonists toward the Taino. He even went so far as to say that the Spanish on the island "are all in mortal sin and live and die in it, because of the cruelty and tyranny they practice among these innocent peoples." Montesino went on to say many other things in his sermon which were recorded by De Las Casas who was a witness:

"Tell me by what right of justice do you hold these Indians in such a cruel and horrible servitude? On what authority have you waged such detestable wars against these people who dealt quietly and peacefully on their own lands? Wars in which you have destroyed such an infinite number of them by homicides and slaughters never heard of before. Why do you keep them so oppressed and exhausted, without giving them enough to eat or curing them of the sicknesses they incur from the excessive labor you give them, and they die, or rather you kill them, in order to extract and acquire gold every day." (Casas, 1552)

The primary policy of the Preaching Friars (Dominican Order) in the New World was to aid and represent the indigenous people under Spanish and Portuguese rule. The initial reaction to this sermon enraged the Spaniards and Admiral Diego Colon (Columbus' son) who promptly had Montesino shipped back to Spain. In Spain Montesino presented his plea to King Ferdinand II. As a result, the king convened a commission that promulgated the Laws of Burgos, the first code of ordinances to protect the indigenous people, regulate their treatment and limit the demands of the Spanish colonizers upon them. The Dominican Order of Friars continued this legacy of protecting the indigenous people, to the best of their ability, for three more centuries.

The cruelty committed by those claiming to be Christians was devastating to the efforts of sharing the Gospel amongst our people. Even today, the horrible history is widely known in both Native and non-Native populations. But it is rare that anyone is aware of the true Believers who stood up for what was right and decried the ungodly actions of the aggressive majority. In America, current statistics reflect that 83% of the population labels themselves Christian. Today, Native Americans comprise less than 1% of the American population. While estimates vary, only 1 to 5% of Native Americans claim the Christian religion. How effective Trickster's (Satan's) plan was! When someone's first exposure to the Son of God is made by men of violence, a lasting impression of extreme repulsion is associated with the Prince of Peace! (Langer, 2012)

Native populations have the highest child and alcohol abuse rate in the nation. These facts make it logical to see how we also have the highest suicide rate in comparison to any other ethnicity in this country. Native Americans have the shortest life spans, lowest levels of education and highest drug abuse rates in the country. (Barnes, 2005) Bitterness, hatred, and hopelessness have become the familiar spirits embraced by First Nations people. It is an utterly foreign concept to live in security or to walk in the strength of forgiveness and love.

Deuteronomy 29:18 *"So let there not be among you a man, woman, clan or tribe whose heart turns away today from YHVH our Elohim to go and serve the gods of those nations. Let there not be among you a root bearing such bitter poison and rotten fruit."* (YHVH -Stern, 1998)

People often express to me their horror at what was done to Native people as part of America's tragic history. I respond by saying, "We may have had it bad for the past 500 or so years, but the Jewish people have had it worse for thousands." It is helpful to me to realize that as awful as it was, I must acknowledge those who had it worse. It is an act of determined gratitude to force myself to see and acknowledge that even within the darkest moments of our people's history, a remnant of our people was saved and remains to this day. A Messianic rabbi whom I highly respect has been heard to point out that he, as a blood born Jew, owns a German made car. If we, as Native people, could be capable of forgiveness, imagine how powerful it would be for every other race of people who has been historically wronged. Taking it even a step further, imagine the individual healing that could take place concerning hurts and wrongs of the past.

I am not downplaying our own Native American Holocaust by pointing this out but rather pointing to a people who experienced an even worse string of tragedies and survived against all odds. The Holocaust of the people of Israel did not begin during World War II. It began when the serpent was kicked out of the garden and the first prophecy was given about the Messiah crushing the serpent's head.

"And I will cause hostility between you and the woman, and between your offspring and her offspring. He will strike your head, and you will strike his heel." (YHVH, 2011, p. Genesis 3:15)

Inquisitions and Crusades are just a small portion of the persecution the people of Israel have suffered. There is a systematic spiritual agenda that spans centuries whose sole goal is to wipe out the Jewish people. As believers in the Tanakh (Old Testament), worshippers of the God of Abraham, Isaac, and Jacob and as born again Christians we should be so close to our Abba Father that the Jewish people are provoked to jealousy of that relationship. Instead, all that has been done is to simply provoke them.

This same provocation spread throughout the First Nations tribes as treaty after treaty was broken. Millions died from smallpox infested blankets that were given by the U.S. Army as silently fatal gifts and at the hands of bloodthirsty soldiers waving an American flag, charging on to "heroically" kill unarmed women and children. The same provocation that is echoed in one of De Las Casas last letters to King Ferdinand rings true for the past five hundred (plus) years as a lasting testimony to the violent evangelism of the "New World:"

"What we committed in the Indies stands out among the most unpardonable offenses ever committed against God and mankind." – Bartolomé de las Casas (Casas, 1552)

The forest engulfed me with its stillness while at the same time washing over me with its gentle songs. It was a bittersweet moment of emotion and memory bundled in sorrow.

"My dad telling me the old stories are some of my favorite memories of him even though the subject matter is difficult." I said to PipeCarrier as he shuffled his legs around in hopes of finding a more comfortable position.

"It is washte that you have good memories of your dad," PipeCarrier replied as I saw a flash of hurt fall across his eyes.

"PipeCarrier, my relationship with my father wasn't always the best. Towards the end, he found his song and he began to mend the sacred hoop between us and the things from the past." I saw PipeCarrier's countenance soften with hope, and I knew I had to open up to him more so that the ground of his heart would be open to hearing my words.

It is important to educate. But even more important than knowledge are wisdom and understanding taught in love. This are how we process that knowledge and how we let it change our perception of matters when we evaluate it to The Creator's plum line of Truth. This is how we incorporate that knowledge into our being and how we make decisions for the future utilizing that learned information. The descendants of the Taino/Arawak people have a powerful spiritual opportunity as the People of First Contact to bring healing, forgiveness and restoration to our other First Nations brothers and sisters so that God can do a powerful work in Indian Country.

Those of us who are descendants of the people who greeted Columbus and who walk in this healing forgiveness need to tell our First Nations brothers and sisters that if we, the Taino, can forgive then they can, too! There they will find the elusive peace that so many First Nations people need, a peace that has been shattered and replaced with hatred that eats away at the heart, mind, and spirit of

First Nations people. While hatred remains in a person's heart, he cannot have peace.

The Native American Holocaust began with the Taino; therefore, let it end with our Taino warriors standing in the gap of reconciliation between First Nations peoples and the Europeans and their descendants. May we all be inspired to live up to the meaning of our name Taino, "The Good and Noble People," by bringing peace and restoration between brothers and sisters by standing in the gap.

2 Corinthians 5:18 *"And it is all from God, who through the Messiah has reconciled us to himself and has given us the work of that reconciliation."* (YHVH -Stern, 1998)

Chapter III: The Green Corn Bvsketv Festival

While the small fire continued to pop PipeCarrier began to sing an old Lakota crow hop song on his hand drum. The smoke caressed the cedar frame while the off-beat rhythm pulsed with his song as my memories now gently glided across my once turbulent inner lake of the past. I was drawn to the beautiful moments of participating in a Muscogee Creek Stomp Dance Arbor tucked away deep in the green swamps of Florida.

I sat on a simple wooden bench made of two tree stumps and one cut piece of log while sharing war stories with the Micco (Chief) of the grounds, a WWII Infantry Veteran. The makeshift bench is what the people would sit on underneath the thatched roof arbor. If they weren't sitting under the arbor then they were out on the grounds dancing. Micco Blue was the chief of a small remnant band of Muscogee Creek people in the Southeast. His gentle voice and compassionate eyes did not hide his warrior's heart.

He was a respected and honored man in his 80's with a strength that defied his elderly body. His hair fell loosely upon his shoulders and was just beginning to accept the random ribbons of grey intermingling with the black hairs.

His dark brown eyes were sharp and vibrant and they would light up when the stomp dance caller would begin to call the dancers to the grounds.

"YeeeeeHooooooooowahhh!

He would answer the call with a powerful "HEEEYYYYY!"

" YeeeeHoooooooowaaaahhhh!"

"HEEEEYYYY!" He would call back with a childlike grin that lit up his glowing face.

His chestnut brown skin, wrinkled with the decades and scarred from the wars, carried untold stories that only Micco Blue and The Creator would ever know. He wore a loose fitting blue and white button up shirt and faded Levi jeans which were tucked neatly into his boots to help keep away the snakes, scorpions, leeches and spiders that surrounded the swampy Stomp Dance Grounds.

I thoroughly enjoyed talking with Micco Blue and will treasure the memory of him and stomp songs forever. The grounds were beautiful with each clan mother preparing their clan areas or food in the cooking chickee (A traditional thatched roof structure where all the meals are prepared). Boys and girls were out hunting, gathering wood, harvesting herbs, or playing. Preparations were taking place around us for the first Stomp Dance that evening.

As the sun began to nestle into its dark blanket the Singer, also known as a Caller, would be encouraging people to come out for the different dances. It wasn't until late in the evening after hours of dancing, when there was only a handful of dedicated dancers left, that the Singer would reach deep into his memories and pull out the songs from the ancient times. Stomp Dance takes you back like a time machine that runs off the songs and shell shakers of its participants. It is one of the most powerful and closely guarded indigenous expressions of thanksgiving and worship to The Creator.

After the Stomp Dancing was over, those who were still awake and had endured to the end met in the thatched roof council house. Often there would be honored guests from other grounds and even other tribes such as Chickasaw and Choctaw. That evening we had some honored guests with us that had shared their laughter and songs in the square. It was at these meeting that the elders spoke and the honored guests would share as well. These meetings would often begin after the sun had peeked over the horizon illuminating the white sand of the stomp grounds.

As the sun began its ascent out of its evening blanket, the last song was sung and the last shell shaker rattled. A short while later, we assembled at the entrance to the council lodge. The elders walked in first and sat in their respective places as the Fire-Keeper made sure the sacred fire was lit in the center of the lodge. Cedar logs stood vertically giving the roof thatched with palm fronds sturdy support and were arranged in a way that it caused the smoke to spiral up within the confines of the logs. The smoke would continue this path up and out the smoke hole in the top. It was during these evenings that the old stories were told and the old prophecies of things yet to come were discussed.

That evening, I struggled within as I heard the elders speak of the things that I had heard growing up in church. An Alabamu elder named Talwa, which means Singer, addressed all of us that evening. As the cicadas sang their songs, Singer shared with us that his people had carried prophecies of things to come for generations. The elder shared that the world would be destroyed by fire, and when this happens the earth will be filled with war. A body of people will appear among the "Indians" that do not belong on our lands. They will be destroyed and then the Great Spirit will destroy the earth to keep others from taking possession of the sacred lands.

Singer slowly made his way down into a comfortable sitting position while still relying on his old walking stick to steady his descent. There were a few moments of silence as a sign of respect for what had just been shared and to show that his words were being thought about. Kowishto', which means Panther, nodded in approval although it was difficult to see him sitting in the shadows of the round house.

Panther, a Chickasaw elder, stood up and stepped into the firelight which revealed his majestic white turban with a pure white egret plume smoothly curving back away from his head. He wore a long shirt with intricately beaded flowers and neatly cinched around the waist with a stomp dance belt that had small sea shells and wood beads braided into its red and blue weave. Although he was smaller in physical stature compared to the others his commanding presence captured every eye and ear in the Round House. Panther's voice almost seemed to purr gently as he spoke. He shared how his people carried a story that the earth had been covered with water.

Creator had come to a man named Nu-u (Noo-uh) and told him to build a large canoe because water would soon cover all the land. Nu-u did as Creator instructed and he built the large canoe that would float upon the great waters. Only one family survived and two of every animal that Creator had led into the giant canoe. He also said that at the time, right before the world is destroyed by fire, it will rain down blood and oil.

I physically shuddered recalling a verse in 2 Peter 3:7 which says, "But by His word the present heavens and earth are being reserved for fire, kept for the Day of Judgment and destruction of ungodly men." This was beyond coincidence so I rested my gaze upon Micco Blue as he braced himself against his walking stick while shifting into a more comfortable position.

Panther gracefully sat back down as the next elder to speak began to stand. He was Achunanchi, which means Perseverer, from the Choctaw Nation. He wore a old black cowboy hat with a long white egret feather sticking out of the back. His ribbon shirt was red with yellow and white ribbons hanging down from the middle of the chest area. A beautiful beaded necklace hung around his neck depicting the official seal of the Choctaw Indian Nation. His smooth voice told the old stories as well as he sang the Choctaw stomp dance songs earlier that evening.

"We know . . ." Perseverer began, "We know that The Creator has destroyed the earth with water once and that fire will come next."

He paused as his patient gaze fell upon everyone. "The story as I was told about the Great Flood, I will share with you so that we remember what happens when The Creator is not happy with what people are doing on the earth. We must be careful with how we treat one another as well as look to walk the ancient path of our ancestors. Then things will be well with our people."

~~~

The Choctaw story of the Great Flood:

In the far distant ages of the past, the people, whom the Great Spirit had created, became so wicked that he resolved to sweep them all from the earth, except Oklatabashih (One Who Mourns for the People) and his family, who alone did that which was good. He told
~~~

Oklatabashih to build a large boat into which he should go with his family and also to take into the boat a male and female of all the animals living upon the earth.

He did as he was commanded by the Great Spirit. But as he went out in the forest to bring in the birds, he was unable to catch a pair of biskinik (sapsuckers), fitukhak (yellow hammers), and bakbak (large red-headed woodpeckers); these birds were so quick in hopping around from one side to the other of the trees upon which they clung with their sharp and strong claws, that Oklatabashih found it was impossible for him to catch them, and therefore he gave up the chase, and returned to the boat. The door closed; the rain began to fall increasing in volume for many days and nights until thousands of people and animals perished.

Then it suddenly ceased and utter darkness covered the face of the earth for a long time, while the people and animals that still survived grouped here and there in the fearful gloom. Suddenly, far in the distant north, there was seen a long streak of light. They believed that, amid the raging elements and the impenetrable darkness that covered the earth, the sun had lost its way and was rising in the north. All the surviving people rushed toward the seemingly rising sun, though utterly bewildered, not knowing or caring what they did. They saw, in utter despair, that it was but the mocking light that foretold how near the Oka falama was at hand, rolling like mountains on mountains piled upon each other and engulfing everything in its resistless course. All earth was at once overwhelmed in the mighty return of waters, except the great boat which, by the guidance of the Great Spirit, rode safely upon the rolling and crashing waves that covered the earth. For many moons, the boat floated safely o'er the vast sea of waters.

Finally Oklatabashih sent a dove to see if any dry land could be found. She soon returned with her beak full of grass which she had gathered from a desert island. Oklatabashih, to reward her for her discovery, mingled a little salt in her food. Soon after this the waters subsided and the dry land appeared then the occupants of the great boat went forth to repeople another earth. But the dove, having acquired a taste for salt during her stay in the boat, continued its use by finding it at the saltlicks that then abounded in many places to which the cattle and deer also frequently resorted.

Every day after eating, she visited a saltlick to eat a little salt to aid her digestion which in the course of time became habitual and thus was transmitted to her offspring. In the course of years, she became a grandmother and took great delight in feeding and caring for her grandchildren. One day, however, after having eaten some grass seed, she unfortunately forgot to eat a little salt as usual. For this neglect, the Great Spirit would not allow her and her descendants from eating salt.

When she returned home that evening, her grandchildren, as usual, began to coo for their supply of salt, but their grandmother had been forbidden to give them any more, and they cooed in vain. From that day to this, in memory of this lost privilege, the doves everywhere, on the return of spring, still continue their cooing for salt, which they will never again be permitted to eat. Such is the ancient tradition to the Choctaws of the origin of the cooing of doves.

What about the fate of the three birds who eluded capture by Oklatabashih? According to the oral tradition they flew high in the air at the approach of Oka falama, and as the waters rose higher and higher, they also flew higher above the surging waves. Finally, the waters rose in near proximity to the sky, upon which they lit as their last hope by perching upside down upon the sky. Soon, to their great joy and comfort, the waters ceased to rise, and commenced to recede. But while sitting on the sky, their tails, projecting downward, were continually being drenched by the dashing spray of the surging waters below, and thus the end of their tail feathers became forked and notched, and this peculiar shape of the tails of the biskinik, fitukhak and bakbak has been transmitted to their latest posterity.

But the sagacity and skill manifested by these birds in eluding the grasp of Oklatabashih, so greatly delighted the Great Spirit that he appointed them to be forever guardian birds of the red men. Therefore these birds, and especially the biskinik, often made their appearance in their villages on the eve of a ball play, and whichever one of the three came, it twittered in happy tones; its feelings of joy in anticipation of the near approach of the Choctaws' favorite game.

But in time of war, one of these birds always appeared in the camp of a war party, to give them warning of approaching danger, by its constant chirping and hurried flitting from place to place around their camp. In many ways did these birds display their kinship to the red man, and he ever cherished them as the loved birds of his race, the remembered gift of the Great Spirit in the fateful days of the mighty Oka falama. (Swanton, 2001)

The details of this ancient flood story are uncanny. The Choctaw Native American accounts that have been passed down orally by the Choctaw storytellers also tell us another story that bears great similarities with the Bible. They say that there was once a time when the earth was one solid land mass. The land looked like a turtle's back as it was rising out of the ocean. It is because of this story that many Native Americans still call the North American continent Turtle Island.

It is passed down that all of humanity was one tribe of people living on Turtle Island and we all spoke the same language until the people decided they wanted to be able to ascend into the Sky World in order to meet with The Creator. The people set about to building a large sky tower that would reach past the stars and into the heavenly realm. The Creator saw what the people were doing and became very upset, so He promptly destroyed the Sky Tower that the people were building. Then the Creator grabbed the land and spread it apart separating many of the people. It was then that the Creator gave people different languages so that they would not come together again in an attempt to rebuild the Sky Tower. (A.Teit, 1917)

With approving nods and a resoundings "Aho" from the others filled the lodge in affirmation of what had been told. The Choctaw elder smiled and made his way back to the spot where he had been sitting on the cool, dry earth. As he lowered himself down to sit Micco Blue slowly stood up and looked at every person that was there and then he graciously thanked the others for sharing their stories. He expressed his concern that the stories would die out and that within generations the very grounds that we stood on would be gone. His concern was the people would not be ready for what was coming because they did not know. Micco had a smooth voice that resounded with gentleness and authority at the same time. His long wispy black and speckled grey hair shone in the fire light as he earnestly spoke.

Micco Blue was afraid that mankind would be caught off guard when these times came. In the old stories, Creator had made man from the dust of the earth by shaping the clay and breathing life into him. This is why the Muscogee name for God is Hesaketvmvse- The Giver of Breath. Once the people had multiplied on the earth, Creator told them many things and about the last days that were coming. Creator told the Muscogee people that fire would destroy the world; people who had long been dead would come back to life, and horrible things would emerge from the earth. There would be a large gathering of people and that death would no longer exist. It is then that the Giver of Breath will seek out those among the people who have lived good lives according to Creator's ways and that Creator would then "take them up." (Grantham, 2002, p. 19)

It wouldn't be until many years later that my acceptance of what was undeniable truth washed over me. I slowly began to realize that Creator had been guiding my path the whole time and blessing me with beautiful memories like this one to go back to and connect with once again.

This was a time of regeneration and thankfulness for the harvest that would capture our focus during those moments at Green Corn Dance. When we would stomp dance we always went counterclockwise because our heart is closest to the sacred fire as we dance. The songs, the dancing, the fellowship and the beauty of ancient traditions make you feel vibrantly alive and connected to an ancient tradition that honors The Creator. I felt exuberant, and Creator's presence was strong. Despite my trepidations and bad influences that wanted to keep me away from church, I realized that I had to accept that the old stories had a connection with the Biblical accounts.

My desire to investigate this more would gnaw at me. The yearning for knowledge and truth helped me to come around full circle back to The Creator. I also realized that through the most trying times of my life, Creator was there all along. Even though I had messed up in my life with poor decision over and over again The Creator remained faithful to the promises made to my mother and father when I was dedicated to God as a baby. That day words of prophecy were spoken over me and I have seen many of them come to pass. The elders say that everyone has a song because God has given each of us a song. That is how we know who are, when we know our song.

In First Nations culture we have a song for everything: Prayer songs, honor songs, ceremonial songs, death songs, horse stealing songs, veteran songs. Songs that lull the baby to sleep and songs that will wake up the bears even songs about how the girlfriend left with the pickup and the dog. But years after they were spoken, despite those words of destiny concerning my purpose, in the darkest hours of my life I thought to myself, "There is no redemption song for me."

Chapter IV: When Surrender is an Act of War

It was in that brokenness of true heart-rending repentance that I understood what Salvation was for the first time in my life. I had come to the altar for as many altar calls as there are stars it seems but this time it was different. Laralyn, the woman who would one day become my beautiful wife, led me to The Lord. People say they found The Lord yet I was acutely aware that He was not the one who was lost. That evening, as my shattered heart cried out for The Creator's purpose for me, the overwhelming presence of pure love filled the room. It was so pure and unconditional that my flesh recoiled as if it automatically understood the depth of its own impurity. I was overcome with the keen awareness of how little I was in comparison to the overwhelming power that a tiny fraction of His presence in the room was generating.

I heard the most loving and gentle voice say to me very clearly, "Make music and point people to me."

Then for a few precious seconds, I was given ears to hear. I could audibly hear the music of heaven! It was the most beautiful symphony I have ever heard and far beyond what I could ever imagine. The purity of each note, the clarity of each instrument, and sound were completely precise. Each beautiful crescendo filled the room with praise to The Creator. There were notes and sounds that I can't describe with the miniscule limits of language. When asked to describe it, the only thing that comes to mind is that the notes were... color. I don't know how else to describe it.

My tears of brokenness turned into tears of absolute joy and exhilaration as I listened to the most supernaturally beautiful music that I have ever heard in my life! I instantly appreciated what I was hearing because I knew that it would not last. I was raised surrounded by incredibly talented musicians which fostered a deep appreciation for music in me as well as a keen ear for singing songs. Music always filled our home; permeated our gatherings; relieved me of early bedtimes; and soaked our culture with joy and life. My early years with music were there to prepare me for this divine calling in my life and for this very day of hearing the music in heaven. For the first time I also asked for a hunger for reading His Word. I prayed that I would feel spiritually hungry whenever I skipped "meals". I truly believe that this is also one of those prayers that The Creator is just waiting to hear.

It wasn't a process or something that took a while to accomplish. As soon as I asked it was instantaneous. I became hungry for His Word, reading it and digging deep into the Hebrew and Greek root words to better understand what I was reading in the Bible. I realized that with my surrender to the Lord, an act of war was declared in the Spirit World. I read in the Scriptures how the Israelite musician warriors went into battle first while playing their instruments of war. I read their stories of victory over their enemies with just songs of praise and blasts of trumpets made of ram's horns. I knew now that my instruments of war in the Spirit World were literally musical instruments. This veteran had traded in his rifle for a drum, his side arm for the bagpipes, and his knife for a flute. As my wife and I studied together, we discovered that all of these instruments were listed in the original languages of Scripture. An old phrase, still used today by many tribes when making agreed exchanges and transactions definitely fit this scenario. Once spoken, it signifies the end of a transaction; the signature on the dotted line. I said, "Good trade."

But even better than trading in weapons of worldly war for those of a spiritual war was the realization that His Son had given His life in trade for mine. What a somber thought! I knew I should honor his memory in a good way. My Native dance to the Son, to honor his sacrifice, would be my life's dance. Every step should be taken in praise. Every time I raise my dance stick will be to honor Him.

Even though my spiritual transformation had taken place, Creator was just getting started with me. There was that ugly root of bitterness, anger, and hatred that was still deeply entrenched in me. Knowing I was called to ministry, I felt that in my current state I would be no more than a hypocrite. How could I speak a message of love with a heart poisoned and fostered by generational hate? I read,

1 John 4:20 *"Whoever claims to love God yet hates a brother or sister is a liar."* (YHVH -Stern, 1998)

Love and hate wrapped up in one sentence. Recalling times when participating in traditional Native American ceremonies, I thought of how many times they are wrapped in a blanket of love but lack depth of the heart. Ceremony with different First Nations tribes showed me the vast difference in the spiritual traditions as well as the similarities. The most striking similarity is the phrase(s) "We are all related" or "We are all connected." The Lakota phrase for this, "Mitakuyasin," has even become cross-culturally spoken and recognized.

Often this phrase is spoken when the prayer pipe is being passed or when entering the ceremonial cleansing lodge. It is an affirmation of our relationship to one another, and yet as I spoke it, I realized my own hypocrisy in making that statement. One is not supposed to lie when you hold the ceremonial pipe yet I began to realize that lying was exactly what I was doing when saying that phrase while harboring hate and bitterness in my heart. As the veil of prejudice was removed from my heart, understanding washed over me like a flood of sunshine when you walk outside on a peaceful spring day. My particular flavor of prejudice was towards the Spanish and the Church because of the devastation my people suffered at the hands of the Conquistadors in the Caribbean and Florida mainland as well as Manifest Destiny which used The Creator as an excuse to take the land... but it spread farther than that.

I felt this bitterness and anger even though I knew that Creator reached out to indigenous people throughout the world including First Nations tribes, and He made Himself known through His works of creation. He valued us as a people, and we loved the beauty of what He had created which is why we call him "The Creator." Even the Bible calls God "The Creator" at least 19 times depending on the translation. Later, He would bring to my mind part of a letter written to Roman citizens almost 2000 years ago by a very revered spiritual leader of his time. His name was Shaul, or Paul as the Romans called him.

Romans 1:20 *'For ever since the creation of the universe His invisible qualities — both his eternal power and His divine nature — have been clearly seen, because they can be understood from what He has made."* (YHVH -Stern, 1998)

Our people knew who the Heavenly Father was, yet Trickster knew how to make us turn away from the Gospel message that came to our shores. The doctrine of conquest left the indigenous people of this land with a poisonous 500 year old root of bitterness, intense hatred towards the church and a feeling of rejection whose end is often found in fast or slow suicide at the end of a barrel, loop of a rope, or the bottom of a bottle. This is how the west was lost, one tribe at a time and still to this day. It is only because of God and His grace that I didn't walk down one of those paths. This new path, the White Path as I have heard some Cherokee elders say is wonderfully straight path that had set me before a wicasa wakan on this cool evening.

A wicasa wakan is a holy man. To me, he was also a good friend and fellow warrior who knew Creator. Wakan Tanka is what PipeCarrier and his people call The Creator which literally means The Great Sacred One in the Lakota language or sometimes the more personal term Tunkasila (Grandfather). PipeCarrier had heard of "Jesus" and knew who He was but he didn't know him as his personal redeemer. I had shared with him what had happened to me on my day of redemption hoping it would be a seed of hope to his spirit that would bear good fruit in the future. However, this is not why we sat across from one another this evening.

Through Creator's guiding steps, I was now sitting across this small, crackling fire on a cool spring night smoking the sacred pipe with my friend PipeCarrier as we shared with one another, and I compared them with the stories in my mind of the Old Ones with the stories that had been written down in the Bible.

Although it is not traditional to write down these ancient stories, without doing so, they stand to be lost with each passing generation. I knew that at some point I had to write them down to ensure that they continue to be told. My inward struggle is that I was taught, like with traditional songs, you do not record them or write them down. This ensure that you have learned the song and have taken it to heart.

Walking the balance between the old ways and living in a modern world can be difficult at times. In this case, the stories are too precious for my bad memory to retell them and I do not want to bring dishonor or disrespect to the elders who confided their stories to me. Knowing my own flaws and limitations as a storyteller I decided that they should be recorded in an effort to preserve them for the next generation. The old stories can help us in our lives and encourage us to forge ahead in the face of adversity. Most importantly we need the reminder of what is coming in the very near future so that we can be better prepared if the fires come in current generations.

Chapter V: Dancing for the Son

The sweet smell of PipeCarrier's personal pipe tobacco blend mingled with that of the fire as we sat and shared songs and laughter with each other. PipeCarrier is exactly what his name declares: one who carries The Pipe, a sacred responsibility and great honor. Now, there are many people who smoke from a pipe. But this does not mean that they are a pipe carrier. There are many people who own a pipe. Perhaps it is a fancy carved pipe with pretty feathers, hanging from a conspicuous place of honor on the living room wall. But this does not make them a pipe carrier. A pipe carrier is chosen by Creator and trained by an elder pipe carrier in all the ceremonial aspects and songs that are a part of this sacred honor.

After carefully making the ceremonial preparations, he had assembled his canupa with prayer and song and we now spoke freely with one another knowing that there would be no lies between us as we held this instrument that is a physical representation of our prayer life. Pure tobacco and herbs are blended together to create a smoking blend called kinnickinnick. Each pipe carrier must pray for his own distinct blend. As I was taught, (and have never heard to the contrary), the smoking blend would not include plants that could make you high or cause you to hallucinate.

To do so would mean that the source of any vision or message you received might have to be questioned. Was it Creator? Or was it the effects of a plant? No, the pipe was a burnt offering for Creator: smoke that symbolically carries our prayers to the Creator. We do not use it for our own pleasure, rather as an offering to the One Who made the plants being burned.

Revelation 8:4 *"on the gold altar in front of the throne. The smoke of the incense went up with the prayers of God's people from the hand of the angel before God."* (YHVH -Stern, 1998)

Herbs are not just burned in pipes but also in smudging ceremonies. Native people typically use four herbs for burning as incense to Creator. Tobacco, sage, sweet grass and cedar were given by Creator to Native people as herbs to use for praying. There are more than just these four but these are widely seen in many tribes across Turtle Island. Each one has its own story as to why they are used. It is interesting to note that the Hebrew word in The Bible for "Intercession" or "Intercede" is "pagah" which at its roots means "to pray with smoke." I wonder how many intercessors in the Church today actually pray with smoke or offer up burned incense to the Lord.

We watched the smoke waft up into the air as the smell of sweet grass and cedar hovered in the air from the few pieces that were burning in the fire. The smell is pure and clean with a welcoming aroma that reminds Native people of home.

"Would you like to hear one of my people's stories?" PipeCarrier asked with a boyish gleam in his eye. The scene was set. The only thing missing was a great story.

Being a traditional Lakota man and Sun Dancer, PipeCarrier began to share with me some of the stories that his grandfather Ghost Dance Boy had passed down to him. This is one of those stories as it was told to me by PipeCarrier, as it was told to him by Ghost Dance Boy as it was told to him by Ghost Dance Boy's father and his father before him . . ..

~~~

The Son Dance

In the long ago time, there was an old Chief of the Lakota people. This was in the time when the Lakota were still on the east coast. The Lakota weren't always buffalo hunters of the plains as most people today have read about in their history books. They were originally located in the east and there is still a remnant of them who can be found there today called the Wacamaw Sioux by some. This story
~~~

takes place before the Lakota were pushed to the west where they are today.

A great and terrible sickness fell upon the land. All of the people were getting sick and dying and no one knew what to do. The medicine men and women tried everything to their deepest knowledge with teas, salves, and ointments made from plants but nothing was working and the People continued to die. As is custom among the People, the old man Chief prepared for his journey to go up the sacred mountain in order to fast and pray for an answer.

The first day the Chief was on the mountain he stood with his weathered arms stretched out towards the heavens and he cried out in a loud yet humble voice.

"Creator! Maker of all things and giver of breath, I come humbly before you on this vision quest. Your people need help! They are dying, and I do not know what to do. We have tried everything that we know and nothing has worked to keep the people from dying. Is there a plant medicine that you can show me how to make a tea or salve that I can then bring to the people to heal them?"

There was no answer…

The second day the Chief stood once again after a full day of singing, dancing, and praying. He looked out upon the land and raised his eyes to the sky and cried out once again.

"Wakan Tanka! Oh Great One! You alone know all things and you are the one who spread the stars out across the sky. Your people are dying, and I do not know what to do. Our medicine people have tried every herb, and our holy men have tried every prayer. Nothing is working and the people are dying. Is there a song that you can give me that I can sing over my people so that they may live?"

There was no answer...

The third day the Chief stood again; although, the hunger had begun to gnaw at his empty stomach, and the thirst was like fire that cannot be quenched. This was to be expected. It did not stop him from his duty to his people and as he stood he looked desperately to the sky for an answer. With hands raised high he called once again upon the Creator.

"Tunkasila..Grandfather! You who are without beginning or end! You who formed man from the earth in the palms of your hands, your children need your help! They are dying, and nothing we have done has worked. Please Creator, is there a dance that you show me that I can pray and war in the spirit realm with?"

There was no answer...

The light of the sun was on its journey to the west as the Chief looked on in awe at the beauty of what Creator had made. With only a small amount of time left before the end of the fourth day, the Chief held out hope that Creator would answer his prayer. He slowly stood with arms raised high and his head facing the heavens. He was over the hunger pangs and was no longer thirsty as his spirit was being fed now through the songs and prayers of the People.

"Great Mystery! You who made the moon and the stars and placed them in the sky, you gave us life and have sustained us throughout the generations. Please Creator, your children are dying, and I don't know what to do other than pray and seek an answer from you. How can my people be saved, oh, Great One in the Sky?"

Just then, Creator sent a spirit being who hovered in the sky above the old Chief who dropped to his knees in awe at this powerful spirit being that appeared before him.

The spirit being moved its arms and with its fingers drew a window in the sky above the old Chief then looked at where he was standing.

"Look through this window, and you will see the answer to your prayers." The spirit said with authority.

The old Chief looked through the large opening in the sky that the spirit had formed. He saw a man who was pierced and hanging on a tree.

The spirit spoke again "He is dying so that your people may live."

The spirit then turned toward the opening in the sky and it began to shrink as the last rays of the sun were being pulled into the western horizon.

"Wait!" the old Chief exclaimed, "What is his name so that we can remember him and his sacrifice for our people?

There is no greater honor among our people then to give your life for another."

The spirit turned to look at the old Chief and with an ageless voice the spirit said, "His Name is Bright Morning Star. Remember His Name." And with those words, the spirit looked to the Sky World and was gone as fast as a bolt of lightning.

The old Chief fell to his knees weeping and thanked The Creator for he knew that his people would be healed.

That's what the old ones say.

~~~

I sat on the cool earth following the trail of fire sending embers into the sky where I was looking up to as if I could see the same messenger spirit that Creator had sent to the old Chief so long ago. I was stunned to hear this story about the spirit that Creator had sent with a dispatch of hope and salvation. I thought of the spirit and what it says in the book of Hebrews concerning angels:

Hebrews 1:14 *"Aren't they all merely spirits who serve, sent out to help those whom God will deliver?"* (YHVH -Stern, 1998)

"So you see, "PipeCarrier said, "This is the ancient origin of the Sun Dance of my people as it was told to me.
~~~

When the old Chief came down from the mountain and told his vision, the People made a dance to honor Creator's Son, Bright Morning Star, who died so the people would live. But over the centuries, the dance has changed."

Poking the fire with the small stick PipeCarrier continued, "We have the Tree of Life, and we dance and sing looking to the sun, and we pierce our skin just as He was pierced. Some tribes Sun Dance without the piercing, but this story is how it all began." PipeCarrier then sat silently as his face furrowed in deep thought. There was pain and rejection in his eyes reflecting from the fire.

"Why haven't these stories been told? God clearly showed Himself to the People," I asked PipeCarrier. I already knew the answer to my own question.

Chapter VI: When Man gets in The Creator's Way

The forest stood in what seemed to be a majestic moment of silence until a lone ember popped from the fire and lazily descended down onto a rock. The crickets began their songs once again and an unseen visitor scurried away in the night as if frightened by the sudden commotion.

"How did you get over the memory of what the church did to your people?" PipeCarrier asked me with a deep longing for peace in his eyes.

I thought about how I would answer him and inwardly prayed that the right words would come out. "I made a conscious decision to empty my poisoned heart's hatred towards the church and towards the "white man". My own seething contempt for them ate me up inside and was destroying my spirit. It had made me a hypocrite. I carried a ceremonial prayer pipe and as a Pipe Keeper repeated praying "All My Relations," not realizing how much of a hypocrite the hatred in my heart had made me. Even when I saw the cross in the medicine wheel"

"Yes, The medicine wheel. This I understand clearly as it is used extensively by my people." PipeCarrier adjusted his body so he was leaning on one arm with the other resting on his knee.

"What did you learn about the medicine wheel, if you don't mind me asking?" PipeCarrier inquired with an intrigued look on his face.

The small fire continued to dance across the wood as the shadows embraced the moonlit forest around us. My memories slowly went back to when I was stationed at Fort Hood, Texas in the late 1990s.

"I was assigned to the 4th Infantry Division and within a week of in processing at Fort Hood, I met a fellow Native who was assigned to the same unit as I was. He was of the Northern Cheyenne Nation, and we quickly became friends."

"There were other Natives who were serving at Fort Hood, and we would all get together in a group and hit the powwow circuit. If we weren't singing on the drum, we were dancing in the powwow circle, all with healthy doses of Indian fry bread tacos, of course," I said while chuckling under my breath.

"It turned out that my Cheyenne battle buddy's grandfather was an Arrow Priest."

I didn't have to tell my Lakota friend what a very honored and sacred position this was amongst the Cheyenne people. There are only a handful of Arrow Priests left.

"Over the course of time, Yamshim, (The Cheyenne Arrow Priest) invited me to a sweat lodge ceremony and to hear the old Cheyenne stories. Yamshim was in his late 70s with long white hair and a kind yet chiseled face shaped from decades of wisdom. His smile was contagious and he loved to joke around with anyone who would listen. His dark almond shaped eyes sparkled when he talked about medicine ways and the old paths, and he was very eager to share the stories of the Cheyenne Nation. It was he who spoke to me in such detail about the Medicine Wheel and the Sacred Hoop."

Yamshim taught me that "We are all related" and "We are all connected" are phrases tied to an ancient symbol that is still used by many tribes to day. It is called the Medicine Wheel or Sacred Hoop. The Sacred Hoop has no beginning and no end. It is the circle of life and represents the Creator and everything that He made. It symbolizes the four directions, the four winds, four seasons of nature and man, and the cross at the center that brings us all together in unity.

The Sacred Hoop reminds First Nations people of our connection in this world and how we each make a difference through our interwoven choices and our actions. It shows us how we are linked in many ways to our natural world and especially to the Creator. It is also reminder of an ancient time when all mankind was one tribe living together on what many First Nations tribes call Turtle Island. The Old Ones prophesied that a time would come when the Sacred Hoop would be broken and that our lives would change forever. The earth will have its greatest shaking and the great waters will flood much of the land.

All of these things are coming because man is not taking care of the earth in the way that the Creator instructed. Mankind's relationship with Creator and one another is in serious disrepair and only through prayer, fasting, reconciliation, and seeking the Creator's perfect plan for our lives can the "hoop" be mended.

Forgiveness is the key to unlocking the healing medicine of closure in our own sacred hoop. The lack of forgiveness in my life caused my relationship with God and people to suffer making my own sacred hoop a broken oval at best. Yamshim always encouraged us to love one another and to live in peace. He instructed me to not say we are all connected just in my head but to say it from my heart and to let it flow from my spirit. Those are a few of the things that he said that still remain fresh in my memory.

Then one day several years later, I read this verse which cut me to my core and brought me to a heartfelt repentance before The Creator:

1 John 4:20 *"If anyone says, "I love God," and hates his brother or sister, he is a liar. For if a person does not love his brother or sister, whom he has seen, then he cannot love God, whom he has not seen."* (YHVH -Stern, 1998)

PipeCarrier and I stared at the fire in silence broken only by the random sounds of crackling embers, singing crickets, and squeaking bats streaking across the night sky. It felt good to talk about these historical and personal hurts to someone else who could relate.

"I understand," PipeCarrier began slowly, choosing his words carefully, "as only a Lakota can understand for we have gone through many of the same things. It began with your people and ended with mine."

He shuffled his feet into a more comfortable position while rubbing one of his numerous battle wounds on his legs.

"Do you know what happened at Wounded Knee?" he asked me bluntly, looking up through eyebrows furrowed with what was evidently pain, although, from the leg he was rubbing or from bullet wounds to generations past, I could not tell.

"I know about the massacre at Wounded Knee and how the people were unarmed when the soldiers came and slaughtered them. They did horrible things to your people and received medals for their actions when all they were doing was dancing and praying," I responded.

PipeCarrier looked at me across the fire with an intensity that was not there before. His eyes glowed wildly, and I was convinced it was from a fire deep within him rather than a mere reflection of the small one between us. "Yes, but do you know the REAL story about what happened at Wounded Knee? What the history books haven't written down?"

"My family was there. My grandfather, Ghost Dance Boy, survived that massacre when his mother covered his small body with hers in order to shield him from the soldiers' bullets. He survived the massacre and told me the story behind the Ghost Dance and what happened when Wovoka the Prophet came to my Lakota people."

There was a mournful silence that followed. I sat patiently waiting for PipeCarrier to continue. Someone raised listening to a storyteller knows not to interrupt the storyteller . . . whether it's during a spoken sentence or a thought. During the pause, I reflected upon how honored I was that Creator had connected me with PipeCarrier. What a treasure he was! What a gift that he would share these painful family memories with me.

PipeCarrier continued, "There was a man called Wovoka the Prophet who was of the Paiute Indian Nation. He was chosen and raised to be a traditional medicine man. As an adult, he was hired as a ranch hand by a man named David Wilson. It was Wilson who taught Wovoka about the Bible."

"One day, during a solar eclipse, Wovoka had a vision. This vision was what birthed the Ghost Dance which was to be held for a duration of five days while the people lived in a righteous way. In Wovoka's vision he said that God gave him clear instructions. God told him he must go back and tell his people that they must be good and love one another, have no quarreling and live in peace with the whites, that they must work, and not lie or steal, that they must put away all the old practices that savored of war, that if they faithfully obeyed His instructions they would at last be reunited with their friends in this other world, where there would be no more death or sickness or old age." (Martin, 2000)

"This expression of dance and prayer was also a way of dealing in a non-violent way with such a drastic change of lifestyle that the frontier time had brought." PipeCarrier followed the trail of a lightning bug as it meandered through the forest. In a sad tone he continued, "It was a good way to deal with the hard times the People were going through. They had nothing else to hold onto."

"Yamshim did tell me a little about the Ghost Dance from his people's perspective," I replied to PipeCarrier as I reach back in my memories to those times.

"What I remember the clearest is when he told me that the Northern Cheyenne called it the "Dance to Christ" and that one time during one of these dances the food bowls kept filling up with buffalo meat. The participants related this story to when the multitudes were miraculously fed fish and bread in the New Testament."

PipeCarrier looked intently at the fire as he replied, "With starvation being such a problem that type of miracle bolstered the validity of the vision that Wovoka was bringing to the People."

Collecting my thoughts on our conversation, I remember reading the book, "Bury My Heart at Wounded Knee" by Dee Brown while I was in college. Hearing the accounts of what happened from descendants of eye witness survivors brings an emotional depth that is hard to convey in writing. Of all the tribes, the Lakota really took Wovoka's vision to heart. They had fought all they could to preserve their rapidly changing way of life.

The Lakota had been rounded up onto the reservations and their weapons and even beading tools had been taken away from them. On December 29, 1890, Lakota Chief Big Foot met four cavalry units who were under orders to capture him. The Lakota raised a white flag in order to signal that they were a peaceful people and they would not fight. Many Lakota were taken up to Wounded Knee Creek where they were ordered to give up their weapons. The medicine man, who was there, Yellow Bird, started singing the song for the Ghost Dance. He did this while urging the others who were there to join him in singing, "The bullets will not go toward you."

One young Native man refused to give up his rifle. Some say that he was deaf and confused as to why the soldiers were physically forcing the rifle out of his hands. Others say that when he saw the soldiers coming for him he fired off a warning shot. The end result is the same regardless of the circumstances right before this cataclysmic time in our nation's history.

Immediately there was confusion and several other warriors pulled out their rifles from under old blankets and began to fire. In the midst of the confusion the surreal beauty of the people preparing to dance was shattered with each thunderous bullet, piercing the delicately hand painted buckskin dresses and shirts with unstoppable force. Since there were no tools available for the women to adorn their dresses with beadwork, they took their buckskin dresses and painted them with crosses and descending doves of peace.

In a somber and distant voice, PipeCarrier whispered, "December 29, 1890 was the day the American soldiers surrounded the Lakota people who had gathered for the Ghost Dance. Never would the Lakota have imagined that the soldiers would open fire on all of them. Over 300 unarmed Lakota elders, women, and children who gathered to pray and dance their prayers to the Creator died that day."

I was then horrified to learn from PipeCarrier that there are pictures that the U.S. Army soldiers took of the abuses they perpetrated upon the women, children, and even babies which they skewered with their bayonets while smiling for the camera. PipeCarrier's voice wavered as tears welled up in his sorrow filled eyes. "Twenty three of those soldiers received Congressional Medals of Honors."

~~~
~~~

I sat in the silence of sorrow listening to this descendant of a survivor retell the story of one of the most horrible events in history of his people. Where was freedom of religion or that all men are created equal? How could it be that the Iroquois Laws of Peace influenced this nation's Articles of Confederation and American Constitution and yet they held no bearing with the indigenous people of this land? (Murphy, 1997)

PipeCarrier looked across the fire at me and continued with an edge to his voice that was not there before. "The newspapers reported it, and they called it a battle instead of a massacre, as they did every time that the Native people were killed and the settlers were victors. The reports said that the Lakota Ghost Dancers were trying to conjure the spirits of our ancestors to come and help them fight against the wacisu [white man]. This wasn't what was happening at all."

PipeCarrier went on to tell me that these Lakota were believers in the message that Wovoka the Prophet had brought. Wovoka had read the Bible and believed everything it said. He brought the message of hope and salvation to the Lakota.

The Ghost Dancers weren't dancing trying to conjure their ancestors' spirits. Wovoka had come and taught the Biblical message of end times. Those Lakota believed that times were so bad, that they must be experiencing the tribulation. The people had gathered to dance and pray with doves and crosses on their clothing. They were filled with the Holy Ghost. According to PipeCarrier's own words, they were doing a Holy Ghost dance and praying that Jesus would return to save them. His vision also included instructions on how the people were to live their lives with The Messiah as an example.

"When the Sun died, I went up to Heaven and saw God and all the people who had died a long time ago. God told me to come back and tell my people they must be good and love one another, and not fight, or steal or lie. He gave me this dance to give to my people." Wovoka

Nobody would have ever thought that a message of love and goodness would turn into something horrible and a stain on the conscience of our nation.

"Can you imagine what would have happened if everyone had known the this part of the story?" PipeCarrier paused letting his question sit with me.

I wondered how many Lakota people had heard this story as PipeCarrier told to me. In an attempt to force assimilate an alien way of life on First Nations people many Biblically based cultural traditions were disregarded as pagan or demonic. How could the drums of our people be outlawed when Creator loves to hear His praise to the sound of the drums?

Psalm 150:4-6 *"Praise God with the drum and dance!"* (YHVH, 2011)

Revelation 6:9-10 *"When the Lamb opened the fifth seal, I saw under the altar the souls of those who had been slain for the word of God and for the witness they had borne. "Sovereign Ruler, HaKadosh, the True One, how long will it be before you judge the people living on earth and avenge our blood?"* (YHVH -Stern, 1998)

I shared these verses with PipeCarrier in hopes that it would help ease his spirit in knowing that God would not allow what happened to go without retribution. I explained to him that God in the Bible righteously hates several things, but one of them on His list is shedding of innocent blood and that His judgment will come.

Years after this, my wife Laralyn and I were in Washington, DC, and we went to the Smithsonian's National Museum of the American Indian for the first time.

One of the highlighted exhibits that day was "Exhibition of Native American Dresses." Laralyn was ecstatic. Some of the most beautiful beadwork, quillwork, and weavings that one could ever see were on display with dresses dating back hundreds of years.

In typical impatient man-fashion, I stopped at each display but really didn't spend much time absorbing and appreciating what I was seeing. There were a few exceptions like the fully beaded saddles and riding gloves crafted with the most intricate and spectacular beadwork I had ever seen.

As I walked through the exhibit, I came around a corner into the next portion of dresses on display. There was a small corridor to walk through but couldn't see what was next. As I kept walking, I was hit with the overwhelming presence of the Holy Spirit. It was so intense that my knees began to shake, and I slowly raised my hand towards the glass and steadied myself as I looked at the dresses enclosed within.

My eyes focused on what was behind the place where I placed my hand on the glass while trying to get my wet-noodle legs to work and read the little plaque above my hand that said: Please do not take any pictures out of respect. I slowly regained my control of my legs; my heart was beating rapidly, and the presence of the Holy Spirit was still there.

My gaze then gingerly fell upon three dresses protected behind glass. They were Ghost Dance dresses! I knew it as soon as I saw them because of the beautiful stars painted along the top, the descending doves from the heavens, and crosses prayerfully painted onto the buckskin. There was no intricate beadwork or incredible quillwork because the government took away the tools needed to be able to make the beauty that the Lakota women would normally have adorned their dresses with.

I stood in awe and then noticed the bullet holes and the stains of blood and at that moment I slowly dropped down on my knees. I had a vision, like I was watching something on TV, of what had happened at Wounded Knee. I saw these women dancing and then the bullets ripping through their dresses. I was overtaken with grief and began to weep uncontrollably. I didn't care who walked by and saw this warrior crying. I felt the heart-rending mourning over what had happened to the women wearing those dresses, yet also recognized the anointing on these dresses that the women had prayed over while they painted and prepared their priestly garments to dance before Creator.

What were their names? Why did this happen? Why was such cruelty executed by the soldiers rewarded with Medals of Honor? These were old men, women, and children who were massacred for merely gathering to dance and pray to Creator for help. Please pray for healing among the Lakota people who are still suffering today and are more impoverished than any other tribe.

These matters become more difficult when prominent people in our nation's history greatly influenced the way that America perceived First Nation's people. Opinions were easily used to sway the masses as did famous author of Wizard of Oz L. Frank Baum. When Baum heard about the massacre at Wounded Knee he promptly published several editorials in the South Dakota Newspaper "The

Saturday Pioneer". The following two editorials show us the inner character of this man whose book has delighted millions of children around the world.

"The proud spirit of the original owners of these vast prairies inherited through centuries of fierce and bloody wars for their possession, lingered last in the bosom of Sitting Bull. With his fall the nobility of the Redskin is extinguished, and what few are left are a pack of whining curs who lick the hand that smites them. The Whites, by law of conquest, by justice of civilization, are masters of the American continent, and the best safety of the frontier settlements will be secured by the total annihilation of the few remaining Indians. Why not annihilation? Their glory has fled, their spirit broken, their manhood effaced; better that they die than live the miserable wretches that they are." (Baum, 1890)

"The peculiar policy of the government in employing so weak and vacillating a person as General Miles to look after the uneasy Indians, has resulted in a terrible loss of blood to our soldiers, and a battle which, at its best, is a disgrace to the war department. There has been plenty of time for prompt and decisive measures, the employment of which would have prevented this disaster. The Pioneer has before declared that our only safety depends upon the total extermination [sic] of the Indians. Having wronged them for centuries we had better, in order to protect our civilization, follow it up by one more wrong and wipe these untamed and untamable creatures from the face of the earth. In this lies future safety for our settlers and the soldiers who are under incompetent commands. Otherwise, we may expect future years to be as full of trouble with the redskins as those have been in the past. An eastern contemporary, with a grain of wisdom in its wit, says that "when the whites win a fight, it is a victory, and when the Indians win it, it is a massacre." (Baum L. F., 1891)

These became the popular opinion of many Americans during these horrific years. Fast forward to a little over a hundred years later, and we can see the end result of all the broken treaties and lies. The following statistics are just for the Lakota Nation which is one out of 566 federally recognized tribes. These are the modern day descendants of the Lakota people who were treated inhumanely by the very government that swore to protect them before Wounded Knee.

On the Pine Ridge Lakota reservation alone: (Foundation, 2010)

- 97% of the population lives below the federal poverty line.
- The unemployment rate vacillates from 85% to 95% on the Reservation.

- Death due to Heart Disease: Twice the national average.
- The infant mortality rate is the highest on this continent and is about 300% higher than the U.S. national average.
- The elderly die each winter from hypothermia (freezing).
- Recent reports point out that the median income on the Pine Ridge Reservation is approximately $2,600 to $3,500 per year.
- Teenage suicide rate on the Pine Ridge Reservation is 150% higher than the U.S. national average for this age group.
- The average life expectancy is 45 years old for men and 52 years old for women
- The rate of diabetes on the Reservation is reported to be 800% higher than the U.S. national average.
- The tuberculosis rate on the Pine Ridge Reservation is approximately 800% higher than the U.S. national average.
- Cervical cancer is 500% higher than the U.S. national average.
- School drop-out rate is over 70%.
- Pine Ridge Reservation schools are in the bottom 10% of school funding by U.S. Department of Education

- 39% of the homes on the Pine Ridge Reservation have no electricity.
- The death rate from alcohol-related problems on the Reservation is 300% higher than the remaining US population even though alcohol sales are prohibited on the reservation.
- 4 out 5 young girls have been abused (physically and/or sexually) by the age of 10
- 3 out of 5 young boys have been abused (physically and/or sexually) by the age of 10.

The fruits being produced by this gnarled tree of injustice is rotten to the core while its permeating its stench into every aspect of American history. What did the elders see and what did they say? Why has their voice not been heard in the classrooms? Eyewitness survivor accounts give us a glimpse into frightening moments in the lives of these peaceful prayer warriors whose descendants struggle each day to live a victorious life in spite of the circumstances.

Black Elk (1863–1950); medicine man, Oglala Lakota: "I did not know then how much was ended. When I look back now from this high hill of my old age, I can still see the butchered women and children lying heaped and scattered all along the crooked gulch as plain as when I saw them with eyes young. And I can see that something else died there in the bloody mud, and was buried in the blizzard. A people's dream died there. It was a beautiful dream ... the nation's hope is broken and scattered. There is no center any longer, and the sacred tree is dead." (Neihardt, 2008)

American Horse (1840–1908); Chief, Oglala Lakota: "There was a woman with an infant in her arms who was killed as she almost touched the flag of truce ... A mother was shot down with her infant; the child not knowing that its mother was dead was still nursing ... The women as they were fleeing with their babies were killed together, shot right through ... and after most all of them had been killed a cry was made that all those who were not killed or wounded should come forth and they would be safe. Little boys ... came out of their places of refuge, and as soon as they came in sight a number of soldiers surrounded them and butchered them there. (Report of the Commissioner of Indian Affairs for 1891, 1891)

This pain and heartbroken emotion can be felt and heard in the voices of the elders throughout Turtle Island to this day. Believers walking in forgiveness should be a driving force behind equal treatment for all people and for turning the hearts of First Nations people away from the bitterness and anger of the past into a place of true peace and solace in Creator. Even if we can illuminate His loving Truth in a person's life for just a split second it is worth it.

Luke 6:31*"Treat other people as you would like them to treat you."* (YHVH -Stern, 1998)

It might make the difference in changing the outlook of one person's life. The American Nightmare is one elders perspective on these bitter fruits and their effect in todays society. We can learn a lot about how to heal the heartbreak by starting to see the world through an elders eyes.

A white man and an elderly Native man became pretty good friends, so the white guy decided to ask him: "What do you think about Indian mascots?" The Native elder responded, "Here's what you've got to understand. When you look at black people, you see ghosts of all the slavery and the rapes and the hangings and the chains.

When you look at Jews, you see ghosts of all those bodies piled up in death camps. And those ghosts keep you trying to do the right thing. "But when you look at us you don't see the ghosts of the little babies with their heads smashed in by rifle butts at the Big Hole, or the old folks dying by the side of the trail on the way to Oklahoma while their families cried and tried to make them comfortable, or the dead mothers at Wounded Knee or the little kids at Sand Creek who were shot for target practice. You don't see any ghosts at all."

Instead you see casinos and drunks and junk cars and shacks. "Well, we see those ghosts. And they make our hearts sad and they hurt our little children. And when we try to say something, you tell us, 'Get over it. This is America. Look at the American dream.' But as long as you're calling us Redskins and doing tomahawk chops, we can't look at the American dream, because those things remind us that we are not real human beings to you. And when people aren't humans, you can turn them into slaves or kill six million of them or shoot them down with Hotchkiss guns and throw them into mass graves at Wounded Knee. "No, we're not looking at the American dream. And why should we? We still haven't woken up from the American nightmare. (Nerburn, 2009)

Please take some time now to pray for the First Nations people:

1) That First Nations people answer the divine calling in their lives.

2) That the shackles of bondage through abuse and drugs be broken off a people who desperately need The Creator to be their Deliverer.

3) That God will send people with a true heart full of love for the people they are called to minister to.

4) For First Nations people to know Yeshua (Jesus) and the power He has to change a person's life who receives Him.

"The fire of hope almost went out; we have to rekindle it," Chief Red Cloud (Mahpiya Luta) Oglala Lakota 1832-1909

Chapter VII: The Cherokee-Principal People of Yah

My thoughts came back to my wife's people. The Cherokee people who live all around us and roughly 45 miles away is the Quallah Boundary which is where the Eastern Band of Cherokee Indians remained after fighting and defending their ancient homeland. The Cherokee have overcome great odds and are a vibrant and thriving people today despite a tragic part of their past.

A lone owl hooted in the distance as if asking us who we were, sitting in his woods so late at night. PipeCarrier and I looked in the direction that our evening friend was hailing from and then I cupped my hands and answered the owl back in "owl language." After a few back and forth exchanges, I didn't hear from him again. I suppose that whatever I said to him in his language was somehow comforting or appropriate.

"The feathers of the owl, or 'mucarro' in my language, are used by the warriors of my people," I said to PipeCarrier who was still looking into the dark forest.

"Did you know that long ago, the Cherokee used owl feathers but they no longer wear them?" I asked PipeCarrier.

"I did not know that. Why did they stop?" he inquired as he tore his fixed gaze from the fire to me for a quick wondering glance.

"A Keetoowah Cherokee elder from Quallah Boundary, Cherokee, North Carolina told me many stories about his people. Out of respect for his family I won't say his name because he has gone home now, but he was a warrior as well. He served in Vietnam and was a survivor of the boarding schools." I said as my memory unlocked the box of fond memories of my Cherokee friend.

I reflected on how we would sing on the drum while traveling the powwow circuit in the Southeast. We shared many good times and hard times as well but one thing that stood out to me was that he was a very forgiving man who loved his people and Creator with all that he had.

"He told me that long ago the Cherokee warriors would wear the owl feathers into battle but after the Trail of Tears they stopped. Now only the bad medicine people use the owl feathers. There is a certain call that the owl does that that is called the death call. When the Cherokee hear this they believe it means that someone is going to die, and it's Creator's way to prepare a person for what is to come. Sometimes a person can pray that death doesn't come while other times it comes and there is nothing that can be done about it."

"Yes, we share the same belief among the Lakota. It is not a good thing to hear the death owl." PipeCarrier replied and shuddered as if he had personally experienced this harbinger of the spirit of death. I imagine he had.

"My Keetoowah friend said that along the route of the Trail of Tears the death owl called its death cry. This is what was passed down by families who survived the forced march to the west. As you know, over one-quarter of the Cherokee Nation who walked the Trail was forever lost on that death march. Ever since then, the Cherokee do not wear the owl feathers. Nowadays, the only ones who do are the witches and bad medicine people. They flaunt the wearing of these feathers with a sense of rebellious pride." I looked across the small fire at PipeCarrier as our eyes locked because we had both met people who were like this and they wreaked havoc everywhere they went. There were also those who wore them out of ignorance, having been disconnected with a people who was once their own, generations ago.

Nodding in acknowledgement of what we were both thinking, I stoked the fire and watch the flames dance on the tip of the stick like my own natural sparkler.

"I hope we are not disturbing our winged-friend's hunt tonight. If we are then we are forcing him to be a vegetarian." We both laughed heartily at the thought of an owl eating a salad and the inside joke. Many Native people joke that "vegetarian" is a Native American word that means "Bad Hunter."

That reminded me of something I brought up to PipeCarrier. "You know, the Cherokee have stories of Kanati, the Great Hunter. But my favorite Cherokee story is one called The Oldest Cherokee Story Ever Told.

"It tells about when a great star appeared in the eastern sky so the Cherokee gathered near modern day Tallulah Falls [located in Georgia] and how spirit beings brought the message to the Cherokee that the greatest Holy Man the world had ever seen was born. They brought stories from across the great waters about miracles this great Holy Man performed.

"But one day, the sky grew dark, the earth shook and the spirit beings came across the great waters crying because this great Holy Man had been killed in a cruel and unusual way. Their tears hit the stones and the stones turned into crosses that can still be found to this day." (Lossiah, 1998)

I paused to see the reaction on PipeCarrier's face as he carefully processed what I was telling him.

PipeCarrier nodded his head and said, "We know the Holy Man that story was about. There are many stories like this that I have heard among other plains tribes."

I imagined PipeCarrier as a little Lakota boy listening to his grandpa tell the old stories and songs not knowing that one day he would be chosen from among his family to carry on the traditional ways of his people.

PipeCarrier looked at me intently across the fire and said with a commanding voice, "You need to write these stories down so they don't get lost. The People need to know these stories. They cannot die with our generation."

I replied while wondering if I would ever sit down long enough to write. "Several books have been written about the possible origins of the Cherokee with a few researchers being convinced they are of Hebrew or at least mixed origin. Have you heard of anything like that?"

PipeCarrier nodded his head in agreement. He lived on Quallah Boundary for a few years, and I could tell by the look on his face that he had heard elders say the same thing I just told him.

I recalled having researched many different perspectives and arguments for the theory of the Cherokee being of Israelite descent. I can only speak from my experiences and memories of when this subject came up around Cherokee elders. Several Cherokee elders from Quallah boundary told me they were descendants of Israelites. It also made me think of what Yeshua (Jesus) said to the religious teachers of his time:

Matthew 23:15 *"How terrible it will be for you, legal experts and Pharisees! Hypocrites! You travel over sea and land to make one convert. But when they've been converted, they become twice the child of hell you are."* (YHVH, 2011)

Was it possible for ancient Middle Eastern mariners to sail across the great waters to our shores? While this may seem farfetched, there is so much we do not know about ancient history. With each passing year, we are unearthing new discoveries that redefine history as we know it. Another possible explanation could be that there was simply intermingling between settlers on this land that predated De Soto and his expeditions in the 15th century. It is widely accepted that the Norse were here and had built villages so why would it be inconceivable to think that other, more advanced civilizations in technology at the time, couldn't have made it over here as well?

As an indigenous person, I find tremendous beauty in archaeological discoveries providing evidence that validates our oral history. Archaeologists have unearthed Hebrew writings on cave walls, stones and more throughout the Americas, some dating as far back as 700 A.D.!

In the early 18th century James Adair, a Hebrew scholar, lived for forty years among the Cherokee. He recorded the similarities within the Cherokee culture, traditions, laws, feast days and more that are similar or identical to the Torah that was given to the Jews and Gentiles at Mount Sinai. A few of the things that Adair recorded go beyond the realm of coincidence in regard to Hebrew influence.

The following are some examples of what he witnessed:

- The Cherokee name for God: YoHeWaH (Yo-Heh-WaH).This is amazing because in Hebrew the name of God is written YHVH and is often pronounced Yehovah, Jehovah, and Yahweh.

- Cherokee name for the Holy Spirit: Loak-Ishtōhoollo-Aba, "the great, beneficent, supreme, Holy Spirit of fire"

- The Cherokee God is a triune that is One being named: El-o-HeyM

- In Cherokee, Au-Do-NiV-Du is the word for "Lord." There is some similarity with the word "Adonai," used by Hebrew-speakers.

- According to the Cherokee story, Creation took seven days and man was made from red clay and woman made from first man's rib. The Hebrew account tells the same, even calling first man "Adam" which means "red earth" in the Hebrew language.

- In Cherokee accounts, there was a great flood which killed the giants but YoHeWah said He would never flood the earth again.

- The Cherokee site the existence of a Patriarch named Aquahami (sounds similar to the Biblical Patriarch Avraham/Abraham).

- The Cherokee kept no idols per their ancient religious laws.

- Six days of work with one commanded day of rest.

- Cherokee considered eating pork unclean.

- Cherokee ceremonial songs often began with singing "Hallel, Hallelu-yah!"
- Cherokee did not practice divination. Being a witch or bad medicine person was punishable by death.
- Cherokee carried a sacred ark before them into battle.
- He states the Cherokee linguistic structure is almost identical to the Hebrew language.
- The Cherokee word for wife is Havah or Avah. "Chavvah" is the Hebrew word commonly translated as "Eve" and means "Lifegiver."
- The Cherokee word for earth is "Yahkane" which means "Yah's footstool."
- New Moon assemblies with the new year beginning at the first sighting of the New Moon during the Spring Equinox.
- In both Hebrew and Cherokee cultures, days are counted from sundown.
- Both cultures had a daily sacrifice of fat including Peace Offerings, Sin Offerings, and Trespass Offerings.
- High Priests of both cultures wear white cotton cloak, 72 bells, a sleeveless jacket, and a breastplate set with 12 stones.
- The Cherokee have Feast Days that closely resemble Passover (Pesach), Feast of First Fruits (Bikkurim), Pentecost (Shavuot), The Day of Atonement (Yom

Kippur) and The Feast of Tabernacles (Sukkot).During the Cherokee Feast that is similar to Passover, the songs include the words – YoHeWahsho Mashi-yo which means The Anointed Ruler in Cherokee.

These are just a few of the examples that show us what could be ancient Hebraic influence among the Cherokee, as enumerated by James Adair. Other accounts that also attribute Hebraic influence of Cherokee society include explorer and botanist William Bartram, James Mooney, John Payne, and Daniel Butrick (who lived with the Cherokee for several decades), to name a few. While the similarities are so striking between the Cherokee and the Hebrew, there are other tribes in the Southeast who also shared some Hebraic similarities in their traditional ways like the Chickasaw, Choctaw, Muscogee Creek, and Haliwa-Saponi. (Adair, 1775) (Starr, 1984) (Payne-Butrik(1830), 2010) Their commonalities were not as detailed as with the Cherokee.

The old stories prophesied the return of the message of their old ways which they thought was what the missionaries brought with them. Unfortunately, the missionaries made the Cherokee stop much of their traditions, calling them ungodly and demonic which is clearly the farthest thing from the truth. If it weren't for dedicated scholars of Cherokee history and the tribal elders and community who were willing to share with these outsiders the old traditional ways, the stories of how the Cherokee walked the White Path would have been lost.

PipeCarrier looked at me intently across the fire and said with a gentle yet commanding voice, "You need to write these stories down so they don't get lost. The People need to know these stories. They cannot die with our generation."

I realized that I had been told stories that had never been written down… and that he was not the only person to tell me that I should write them. They could die with me if I didn't put them to paper. Some of the stories were things that we personally went through we often share when ministering.

"PipeCarrier," I asked as I tipped my head back and slightly to the side. "Remember when we set up the drum on the island in Cherokee?"

"Yes, I remember that day clearly," PipeCarrier replied with a huge smile on his face. "That was a powerful day on the reservation. How did that all get started anyway?"

"I was hoping you would ask." I said with a large, cheesy grin on my face.

Chapter VII: Expanding the Boundary of Quallah

One year, Creator planted a vision in my wife Laralyn's heart, for us to take a small group of people with the drum to the Cherokee reservation in North Carolina to sing and proclaim the Gospel in a culturally contextual manner. I knew this could be a difficult assignment because the prevailing religious institutions on Quallah Boundary (the Cherokee reservation) teach against drums, dancing, and other cultural expressions of worship. This is not the case for the entire reservation as there are exceptions of those who are willing to do what is written in The Bible over what is sanctioned by man.

It is unfortunate that some denominations called to the reservation teach that men's hair must be short, going to a powwow is a slippery slope to hell, the drum is evil, and Native dances are not to be done. We have personally experienced this doctrine in the church from leadership across denominational lines but mostly on reservations throughout the country. It's amazing how we can meet people from the same denominations outside of the reservations and they are appalled at the thought of that doctrine.

Although there are several churches in Quallah there are many people outside of those church walls that only others in the Body of Messiah can reach. Our efforts were not to step on the toes of the ministries that have worked tirelessly among the Cherokee. Our goal was to find those that those ministries couldn't reach and then get the people plugged into their local church on the Boundary for further discipleship. We tried to coordinate a meeting with the Principal Chief to get his permission to set up on one of the islands along the Oconaluftee River. Receiving permission is crucial and not to be taken lightly. Even if it takes years, be patient and wait for that door to be opened so that your efforts are not seen as a crusade or invasion.

The evening before the outreach, my son Michael and I, were privileged to spend time with William Mervin Mills (Oglala Lakota) who is a former U.S. Marine and winner of an Olympic Gold Medal for the 10,000 meter run in 1964. We shared some laughs, and I was honored to pray for him before the evening was over. Several of us veterans were there to bring in the flags for the event and I felt confident and hopeful about the rest of the weekend. I couldn't wait until the next day!

Opposition appeared like a flash flood right before our outreach event when I was told at the last minute that we needed a permit to be issued by the Cherokee government. Any type of event that takes place in the park needs this permit. Without it we would not be able to set up a drum in the park and sing. So, I awoke early the next morning to go meet with the Chief of the Eastern Band of Cherokee. Unfortunately, the tribal office parking lot was completely empty. The doors were locked to all of the offices, so a little panic set in. I spotted some women getting into a car, and I asked them what was going on that the tribal offices were closed. They told me a Tribal Council member had passed away, so all the offices were closed for the day.

I was stunned. We had put the call out to many people to meet us on the reservation for this outreach. People were driving from different states to come meet us, but without permission and a permit to set up from the Chief, we wouldn't be able to do anything. Naturally, it was at this point that I began to question whether or not this plan was the Lord's. There is a spiritual principle that to be blessed by the authority over the land to minister to the people is important. Most mission teams have the right heart attitude when going to a reservation, but they find that they are unable to connect with the people they are there to help. Relationship is crucial in Native American communities and few ministries nurture this vital component. We are a living, loving, and hurting people who amount to more than a salvation notch on an evangelical belt. Proper protocol is rarely done yet it is a key that opens the flood-gates of heaven in a ministry to any tribal people group. Yeshua (Jesus) once taught:

John 10:1-2 *"Yes, indeed! I tell you, the person who doesn't enter the sheep-pen through the door, but climbs in some other way, is a thief and a robber. 2 But the one who goes in through the gate is the sheep's own shepherd."* (YHVH -Stern, 1998)

Beyond the need for a paper permit, this type of authority given in the Spirit World is crucial to receive from the Chief's in order to minister to his people. He holds an authority over the land, and we wanted to be welcomed in through the sheep's gate to do the Shepherd's work so that it would bear good fruit. While we had understood the concept of gifting and protocol as Native people, it was only recently, at this point, that we'd begun to apply the principle to ministry, having recently read the book Warfare By Honor: The Restoration of Honor: A Protocol Handbook, written by Qaumaniq (Author), Suuqiina (Contributor).

Anyone interested in ministry to Native people should understand the principles of proper protocol described in this book. Receiving this blessing through proper protocol opens doors so that your work can bear more fruit, or in some cases, any fruit at all.

I sat down on a little bench after walking from door to door hoping that someone might still be there, but it was all to no avail. Trickster began to speak in my ear telling me that it was all for nothing. People were going to be mad that they spent their time and money on this mission trip and that maybe Laralyn had heard wrong from God.

I picked myself up and refused to listen to the lies of the enemy as I knew beyond a shadow of a doubt that Creator had instructed us to do this. I sat in the shade of a cool tree on that little bench and I prayed. "Creator, I know that you have set all this in place and I believe that you will work this out. If this is a test, I do not want to fail you, but I don't know how I'm going to get permission and the permit to do your work on this reservation. There has been resistance from the enemy to us being here even before we stepped foot on Quallah Boundary, but I know that you sent us here for a reason. Please, open the doors for us to do this according to your way and in the right way. In Yeshua's name I humbly ask this of you, Amen."

I felt like God was telling me to go and sit on the steps to the Chief's office and wait. So, I got up and walked over to the steps. I breathed the beautiful Appalachian mountain air as a wave of peace fell over me like a warm blanket. While I listened to the birds singing their songs, I knew that everything would be ok. Then I saw a car pull up into the parking spot directly in front of me at the Chief's office!

My heart started racing but I quickly saw it was not the Principal Chief. Another man had gotten out of the car and he walked towards me saying, "Hello, is there is something I can help you with?"

"Yes sir" I replied, "I had an appointment to get permission and a permit from the Chief to do a ministry outreach over at Oconaluftee Park, but I heard about the what happened to one of the Tribal Council members. I'm sorry for your loss."

The Cherokee man looked at me and asked," What type of outreach are you doing?"

"It's an outreach," I quickly replied not knowing where this was going, "for everyone on the reservation from the youth to the elders. Helping people to connect with God so that their lives can change for the better and to ignite the fire of hope in people's lives who are hurting or going through struggles in their lives whether it is addictions, abuse, or whatever is holding a person back from being whole."

The man looked at me and it felt as if he was searching my heart. "Follow me inside; I think that I can help you."

The smile on my face was huge! God had made a way. As I followed the man inside, he led me to his office where I read the plaque on his desk: Vice-Chief. I was overjoyed at how awesome God is and how He was there the whole time.

The Vice-Chief took out a paper and begin to sign it when he looked up at me and said, "I had forgotten something in my office and I don't believe in coincidences. I'm also not one that is a regular church goer but I do know that it was God's grace that had me pass out one night face up in the water instead of face down. Here you go, son and thank you for what you are doing for our people."

I was overjoyed and overwhelmed at what had just happened. Only Creator could have orchestrated this to happen this way. The enemy opposed this little mission trip but Creator prevailed. It reminded me of what Shaul (Paul) had written in his first letter to Corinth:

1 Corinthians 16:8-9 *"I'll stay here in Ephesus until the Festival of Pentecost. In spite of the fact that there are many opponents, a big and productive opportunity has opened up for my mission here."* (YHVH, 2011)

People began to steadily arrive and we set up the big powwow drum in the middle of Oconaluftee Park. The air was cool, the birds were singing, children from every walk of life were playing in the river, and there was an excitement in the air as we prayed that the Lord's perfect will would happen that day and that no ravens would snatch the seeds that we were planting that day.

My wife, Laralyn, with her artistic flair, had made poster signs that said things like "Samson had long hair," "Drum & Dance = Biblical" (with accompanying verses Psalm 150:4), "Praise God with drum and dance!" and Psalm 149:3 "Let them praise his name with dancing"), another sign said "Jesus is Tribal." Volunteers stood by the road with these signs and many prayed for people who were walking down the sidewalks. The signage may seem strange to some, but in Indian Country the church missionaries told (and some still tell today) native people that singing on the drum and dancing was demonic.

One elder, who was with us, survived the church-run boarding schools whose motto was "Kill the Indian, save the Man." As a young student at that school, whenever he spoke the Cherokee language, the priest or nun in charge would drive needles through his tongue while telling him he spoke the language of demons. What a beautiful act of forgiveness that he was able to overcome the pain of that abuse and to disconnect, in his mind, God from the horrific acts of abuse he experienced at the hands of people claiming to be doing the will of God.

Let's recall for a moment that Ezekiel 28:13 alludes to Satan being a part of the music in heaven. Some interpret this to mean that Satan was the worship leader in heaven; although, the Bible doesn't precisely tell us this. According to the book of Ezekiel, his pre-fall body was comprised of several instruments which is why some Christian denominations only worship with vocals, no instruments. If one can make a blanket statement, as a whole, First Nations' culture is infused with Creator in everything that we do, especially our songs and dances which are a way of praying and worship. We have songs of war, honor, victory, praise, worship, prayer, and more.

It makes sense that the adversary wanted to take that away from us. Not only would that work to destroy our identity but it would also go far in making us believe that our Heavenly Father made a mistake when creating us. Making us believe our cultural expressions of worship are evil is destroying our unique expression to Creator from within the global corporate Body of Messiah.

In John's vision, recorded in the book of Revelation, it is interesting to note that he saw people of every nation, tribe, people, and language. How would he have known this unless the people were culturally identifiable in some way? It is apparent from this Scripture that in some way or another, when we are in these glorified bodies, we somehow retain aspects of our earthly ethnic cultures.

Revelation 7:9 *"After this, I looked; and there before me was a huge crowd, too large for anyone to count, from every nation, tribe, people and language…"* (YHVH -Stern, 1998)

The Body of Messiah is to be unified, but we are not clones. We won't all be praising and worshipping in English and we won't all look the same. The Body of Messiah exemplifies Unity with Diversity, and we see this in Yochanan's (John) vision in the Book of Revelation.

It is quite obvious from this verse that we retain our earthly culture and language in Heaven. Otherwise, how could John have realized that the people were from different nations, tribes, and languages? I remember an African brother who was at the park that day who couldn't wait to come to worship with the Cherokee at a reservation church. He was sorely disappointed because there were no drums, rattles, or dancing nor was there the accompanying joy of the Lord that contagiously spreads when worshipping Him the way He created us to worship. This gentleman said he would love to take some of the Cherokee people he met and bring them to Africa so they can see how they worship with their drums, congas, rattles, shouting, and dancing.

So there we were in Cherokee setting up my family drum. The male singers took their seats and prayed as the women singers gathered around, agreeing in prayer. We prayed, as is protocol when singing at the drum, that together our voices would glorify Creator and that He would draw those who were ready to hear His message of salvation. We prayed that healing would begin in the hearts that heard our songs. We began singing songs, some old and some new, while keeping the steady rhythm of the drum, the heartbeat of our people, going. The songs change and the beat changes based on the songs.

I do not like it when people call our songs "chants." While the word "chant" comes from an old French word "chanter" meaning "to sing, celebrate," unfortunately, the same word is used as a root for the word "enchant" which has obvious occult ties. It is a way of implying that our songs are something other than what they are. But listen closely to our songs and so often you can hear the name Yahweh being called. Even the ancient Native American songs sing His Holy name.

Colossians 3:16 *"let the Word of the Messiah, in all its richness, live in you, as you teach and counsel each other in all wisdom, and as you sing psalms, hymns and spiritual songs with gratitude to God in your hearts."* (YHVH -Stern, 1998)

The drum always draws crowds of people, and soon there was a large group of people who had come to the drum. The listeners were enjoying the singing and snapping pictures. As I looked over the drum at the onlookers and stood to preach the Gospel, I saw before me a multitude of nations, tribes and tongues: African, Hindu, Irish, Cherokee, Mexican, and more! I began to teach about how the Cherokee knew YoHeWaH and spoke the words that the Holy Spirit prompted.

As I spoke, I noticed a small group of Cherokee teenagers who had sat down at the front and were intently listening. I told them that they could dance; they could sing on the drum, and they could be Cherokee and be a believer!

After I finished speaking, several people came up and asked questions about The Lord. Others were intrigued and had never heard The Gospel preached the way it was, calling Jesus by His tribal name Yeshua, pointing out that He was of the Tribe of Judah, of the Clan of David and that He was a tribal man, a Holy Man.

There was a Cherokee elder who was there, and she slowly walked up and held out her weathered brown hands that were fitting to a traditional potter or basket maker. She looked at me through her dark, almond eyes and said, "Thank you," her voice quivered as tears began rolling down her eyes, "I didn't know that I could be Christian AND be Indian."

It was moments like these that filled my heart with joy, and, as I watched her walk away, I noticed a middle-aged Cherokee man who was leaning up against a large tree watching what was transpiring. He was tall with short dark hair and light brown skin. The Holy Spirit told me to go talk to him, so I began walking towards him. I noticed that others on the mission team were talking with people and Laralyn was over speaking with a couple from India.

I walked up and said "Siyo, how are you doing, man?"

"I'm all right, just watching and listening to the songs on the drum," he said with the typical Appalachian Chero-kee accent found on the Quallah Boundary.

"Do you want to come join us? I've got some extra drumsticks. You are more than welcome," I asked him by the prompting of the Holy Spirit. You see, not everyone can come and sit at the drum to sing. It is considered a sacred instrument of worship with several protocols that have to be observed by the singers, the Lead Singer, and the Drum Keeper. It is the Lead Singer and Drum Keeper's call if someone is brought to the drum, and this was the only person we met that day who I was prompted to invite to the drum.

He looked around nervously as if someone might be watching and then his countenance fell and he lowered his eyes to the ground. I felt his heart grow heavy as he began to speak.

"I used to sing on the drum, and I used to dance at powwows. I was a champion dancer and singer and used to go throughout the Southeast with our drum to powwows. Then I got caught up with drugs and drinking too much, and I started to make a wreck of my life. It was really beginning to affect my family, and I knew I had to stop this destructive lifestyle." He sighed as if weighing his words carefully before he continued.

"I went to a local church and told the preacher man I needed to change my life. I asked him what I needed to do." He paused again, struggling with a distant memory then he took a deep breath as his next words came out filled with pain.

"The preacher told me that I needed to pray a sinner's prayer and accept Jesus, so I did. Then he told me that I needed to cut off my long hair and stop being Indian otherwise he wouldn't baptize me."

"I didn't know, and I trusted him so I took some scissors and cut my hair like he said. I went home that day and as soon as I walked through the door my family looked at me and screamed, 'DAD WHAT HAPPENED TO YOU?!'"

"I told them what I did and what the preacher man said I needed to do. They were so upset! They told me they NEVER wanted to step foot into a church and if I was going, it would be alone." Another deep sigh escaped from this pained Cherokee man as we stood there.

Yet again, here I was embarrassed for the Lord by the actions of a well-meaning but unknowingly-misguided brother-in-the-Lord. I wondered how often this type of thing had happened. It was small wonder that Native people believe Christianity to be "the white man's religion" when they hear that you have to stop being Native in order to convert. This could not be farther from the truth! In fact, the culture of the Bible was very tribal. The Son of God Himself was always using agricultural stories to convey important life lessons to all who would listen. Using examples of the earth was commonplace in Native culture, as well. If anything, tribal mentality gives one a head start in understanding the culture of Scripture.

"Would you like me to pray for you? Do you need prayer, brother? I'm sorry that this happened to you. It's really not an accurate representation of the church." I couldn't imagine the depth of his pain but I could see it in his dark eyes and in the slump of his defeated shoulders.

He took a deep breath and looked at me, "No, I'm ok. I'm good with God now, but I'm worried about my family. My wife and kids, they want nothing to do with God. I just want them to be saved and baptized, to know God. Can you pray for that?"

"Absolutely!" We both stood under the shade of the large tree, and I prayed for his family to be healed from the emotional pain that came from his experience. We agreed together in prayer that his wife and kids would come to know Yeshua (Jesus). We prayed for wholeness and restoration in his divided family and peace that only God can give to a torn and hurt family.

Tears were rolling down our cheeks and flowing down our faces like the Oconoluftee River. He turned to leave and with hope in his voice, said in Cherokee "Sgi tso-s-da-da-nv-tli(Thank you my brother). I walked back to the drum, and we resumed singing. The rest of the day involved cycles of singing, preaching, and praying as crowds of people would gather. We enjoyed praying for people, counseling them, answering their questions, and planting seeds we hoped would bear much fruit in fertile soil.

During one of these sessions, a small group of Cherokee teenagers came and sat down at the front of the crowd, listening intently. They seemed very curious and sat very still as I was led to speak about how the Cherokee knew

God and walked in His ways, of how the drum and dance were used to honor Him instruments of prayer, praise and giving thanks.

Exodus 15:20 *"Then Miriam the prophetess, Aaron's sister took a drum (תֹף = toph) in her hand, and all the women followed her, with drums (תֹף = toph) and dancing."* (YHVH, 2011)

Psalm 150:4 *"Praise God with drums (תֹף = toph) and dance!* (YHVH, 2011)

Psalm 81:2 *"Begin the music, strike the drum (תֹף = toph)…"* (YHVH, 2011)

What has been translated as tambourine, timbrel and tabaret in most bibles is the Hebrew word, תֹף (toph), which literally means drum. One of my favorite verses gives us a mental picture of The Lord going to battle to the sound of the drums and harps.

"Every stroke the LORD lays on them with his punishing rod will be to the music of the drums (תֹף Toph) and harps, as he fights the battle with the blow of his arm." Isaiah 30:32 (YHVH, 2011)

The Cherokee youths paid close attention to my words concerning how the Lord commands us to dance, sing, and beat the drums in a way that honors Him in warfare and worship. After I finished talking about these things, I felt the Holy Spirit wash over me once again, and I asked if anyone wanted to start a new life in Messiah. I asked if any of the Cherokee who were there wanted to accept Him into their hearts, and immediately two of the young Cherokees stood up. A teenage girl and her brother walked up and told me they wanted to accept Him and walk in His ways.

I was overjoyed and said to them, "The sacred river of your people, the Oconaluftee, would be a perfect place to be baptized. Are you ready?" I looked over my shoulder at the river flowing just feet away from where we stood.

They both looked at me with eager anticipation and agreed. I asked a brother in the Lord to help with the baptism since he was one of the few local Cherokee pastors who embraces his heritage as well as the Bible. We had involved him from the beginning since we knew that it would be important to connect people to a local church where they could be fed and discipled.

We started to walk toward the river in preparation to get into the cool living waters. We walked out into the refreshing, flowing waters of the Oconoluftee River, to a spot that was the perfect depth for a full immersion. Then I looked up to the shore. Standing there was the Cherokee man I had spoken to earlier looking at us in the water. The young girl followed my gaze and called out to him with a huge smile on her face while excitedly waving both of hers hands in the air. "Dad! We are getting baptized."

I looked at her and said "That's your dad?" It was an impulse response from shock even though I knew it was him. I was witnessing his prayer being answered right before my eyes – a prayer that had been prayed and agreed upon THAT VERY DAY! Joy and amazement at the goodness of our God swept over me like the river where I stood.

I motioned for the father to come into the water and be a part of the baptism. By the end of that day, his children had been baptized, and they began going to church together for the first time. Isn't Creator awesome? It is no wonder that Awesome is one of His names because He does things that are mind boggling! Yet I couldn't help but wonder what the outcome would have been if I had given up on getting that permit earlier that very morning.

Throughout this whole day, The Creator was glorified, and He didn't just show up at the last minute, as many people like to say. No, He was there the entire time. As a result of His presence, Salvation (Yeshua) came to some of the people of Cherokee, North Carolina that day, as well as for several others who were visiting. Some people renewed their already established faith.

At the end of the day, we marveled that one act of obedience can produce eternal fruit for another person but we may never know unless we step out of the boat and have faith that we will walk on those turbulent waters.

~~~

"I have always believed that the Great Creator had a great design for my people, the Cherokees. I have been taught that from my childhood up and now in my mature manhood I recognize it as a great truth. Our forces have been dissipated by the external forces, perhaps it has been just a training, but we must now get together as a race and render our contribution to mankind. We are endowed with intelligence, we are industrious, we are loyal and we are spiritual but we are overlooking the Cherokee mission on earth, for no man nor race is endowed with these qualifications without a designed purpose..." Red Bird Smith-Kituwah NightHawk Society (Thomas, 1953)
~~~

Chapter VIII: Fathers, Hide Your Daughters

The fire was slowly fading so we occasionally dropped a few dry pine cones and small twigs into it in order to keep it lit for the soft light it emitted. My mind was racing, full of all the things PipeCarrier and I had been talking about this evening. I knew that I wouldn't remember all of our vast conversation, which had spanned many moons of our lives. I gazed into the fire and knew, felt, sensed deep in my inner being that things were not getting better with mankind and that we were delving closer to the edge of destruction.

Elders from First Nation's tribes had received prophetic visions of things to come thousands of years ago. The Hopi said that when the spider's web covered the earth, it was close to the time when the fires would come. According to the Mohawk Prophecy of the Seventh Generation, seven generations after contact with the Pale Faces, the Onkwehonwe (Real People) would see the day when the trees would die from the tops down. The prophecy said that strange animals would be born deformed or without limbs. Huge stone monsters would tear open the face of the earth. The rivers would burn as if water could catch on fire. The air will become harmful and burn the eyes of man.

According to the prophecy of the Seventh Generation, the Onkwehonwe (Real People) would see a time when the birds will fall from the sky and fish will be found dead in the waters. Mankind will come to express remorse for the way that he has treated what Creator entrusted us to care of. The last part of the prophecy is that after seven generations of living in close contact with the Pale Faces, the Onkwehonwe would rise up and demand that their rights and stewardship over the earth be respected and restored. Support will come from men and women that will come to the Onkwehonwe, to the eastern door of the Iroquois Confederacy, for guidance and learning. Great turmoil will engulf the earth after these things come to pass, and there will be great battles where many will perish.

We are now seeing the trees are beginning to die from the top down in the west(acid rain); the stone monster tearing up the land could be construction equipment; air pollution is becoming a serious health risk and is tied into the acid rain as well; polluted rivers have burned from oil or other toxic waste that have been dumped into it, and deformities in animals and human beings is become widespread. Could these be the interpretation of these ancient prophecies?

We are to look for these signs so we know that the times of the fires are coming soon. When we see these things we must begin to prepare and teach our children how to survive in the face of great adversity. It is this present generation of youth of the Kanienkehaka (Mohawk) to provide the example and leadership needed to help people during these difficult times. Love between people will grow dim like a dying fire and there will be times of hardship and testing. The children of the Kanienkehaka (Mohawk) are the seventh generation spoken of in these old prophecies.

The Cheyenne said that when the buffalo cover the land once again, the time is near for the fires that will cleanse the earth. Not only have buffalo numbers increased across this land, but their images have covered the nation when the buffalo nickel was recently reintroduced, newly minted by the U.S. treasury in 2005. (Wolk)

The virtual spider has spun its worldwide web across the planet. Even the physical web of electrical and telephone wires has spun its way around our world, suspended on dead trees we call telephone poles. These three prophecies have come to pass in our lifetime with several more that have yet to happen.

Yeshua (Jesus) said: Mathew 24:37 *"As it was in the days of Noah, so it will be at the coming of the Son of Man."*

In the days of Noah, people were bustling about in their everyday lives, ignoring the dire warnings being given by Noah about God's impending judgment. The people laughed at Noah, mocked him and couldn't believe what he was saying because they had never experience anything called rain. When the floodgates opened, prophetic fulfilment was quick and destructive. Settled in the complacency of everyday living, many died that way. The earth has been baptized by water and what remains is its baptism of fire.

I realized that the Word of God had become real and alive to me when I started being appalled at nursery décor depicting various happy-faced animals floating on a cartoon ark. There were no smiles on earth that day. How horrendous and terrible that day was for mankind! I know Noah could hear the people screaming and drowning while they tried to claw their way into the ark, begging to gain entrance into the very object of their ridicule. It was a heartbreaking time in collective human history. The world was forever changed and only eight people were saved.

Rarely do we hear why the Creator destroyed the earth with water. I turned my attention back to PipeCarrier, whose war scarred face was showered with moonlight as it cascaded down his back as if tracing the length of his long black hair and asked him, "What do you know of the star people?"

PipeCarrier focused his gaze beyond the moon into the deep evening sky full of shining stars. He pointed to The Warrior constellation's belt and said. "They fell from the heavens in the ancient times. They took our women. They were not washte [good]."

PipeCarrier confirmed what I have heard from many other tribal elders. My father told me that there was a great battle in the Sky World where good spirit and bad spirits were fighting one another. The bad spirits were thrown from the heavens down to the earth below where they made themselves out to be gods.

These star people took our women by force and the resulting children became the race of giants that we read about in historical accounts from cultures around the world, including the Bible. Interestingly enough, the repeating similarity is these beings came from the sky, took the human women, and produced a race of giants.

When I served in the U.S. Army, I met a traditional Navajo woman whose family was of the Bitter Water and Towering House Clans. We were on guard duty together one evening when we were deployed out in the desert, and we began talking about the star people. The most famous of the Southwestern star people is Kokopelli. This figure is well-known in pan-Indian Native American art and even common art that can be found in national retail stores although its origin is in Southwest United States.

Kokopelli is one of the star people who fell from the heavens to the desert region of the Southwest, according to native tradition. He quickly made himself out to be a god of rain and fertility demanding worship and tribute of a young woman in exchange for bringing the rains to the fields or fertility to women by playing his flute. In the older renditions of him, he is often depicted with a hunched back, four protrusions sticking out of his back and two arms holding a flute which he would play to lure women to himself.

Sometimes in more modern depictions, the four protrusions are what look like four crazy dreadlocks poking out from the top and back of his head. There are even many of the ancient drawings that depict him with an erect phallus, alluding to the sexual nature and focus of this false god. His portraits are not just found in the Southwest; there is even a petroglyph carving of Kokopelli on the island of Puerto Rico where he visited the Taino Native Americans.

The stories of Kokopelli are vast across many Native cultures. It is strange to me that this seducing spirit could have grown in such popularity across the country. It is crucial that we know the origins of the things that we have or decide to pass along to another generation. For some time as a child, my wife lived on the Navajo reservation in Shonto, Arizona where an old song is occasionally sung:

"Fathers, hide your daughters; Kokopelli is coming!"

Kokopelli is just one of many "star people" that fell to the earth and made themselves out to be "gods." There are numerous accounts of giant tribes that sprung forth as a direct result of these fallen ones mixing with the human women. The common thread in the many cross-cultural stories across the globe is that these beings taking human women and breeding a race of giants. It is found throughout the world; so many cultures have stories that have been passed down for thousands of generations centering on these giants.

If you are a believer in the Bible, yet find yourself incredulous at the mention of this subject, ask yourself why? Either you do or do not believe the Bible when it says in Genesis 6:1-4:

Genesis 6:1-4 "*6 When men began to multiply on the face of the land and daughters were born to them,*

2 The sons of God saw that the daughters of men were fair, and they took wives of all they desired and chose.

3 Then the Lord said, My Spirit shall not forever dwell and strive with man, for he also is flesh; but his days shall yet be 120 years.

4 There were giants on the earth in those days—and also afterward—when the sons of God lived with the daughters of men, and they bore children to them. These were the mighty men who were of old, men of renown.

In Genesis 6, we clearly read that these races of giants covered the earth. It distinctly tells us that the fallen ones looked upon the women and wanted them so they took them, had relations with them, and from these unions the giants were born.

Why is this subject not discussed in churches and Bible studies? Are we to be multiple choice believers, picking and choosing what we want to believe concerning the Word of God? Heaven forbid! For centuries the skeletal remains of these giants have been systematically unearthed. In America, we find countless newspaper articles and reports detailing skeletal remains of these giants ranging from seven to twelve feet tall, and in some rare instances even larger.

For the scientific community at large to admit the existence of these skeletal remains means two things: First, that evolution, as it is currently presented, is wrong. And secondly, that the physical evidence gives credence to Scriptural accounts of giants since it validates what was written thousands of years ago by Moses, inspired by God. One semester, my Archaeology/Anthropology professor was doing a lecture on Native American "legends" and began talking about the Muscogee Creek Indian stories that centered around Este-Papv (Ishtee-Papa). The professor was telling us that the stories are talking about a mountain lion which is not what the stories are about.

Este-Papv in the Muscogee language means "Man-Eater." This "Man-Eater" lived in a cave and was a giant who frequently raided villages and would decapitate the warriors who tried to kill him. Then "Este-Papv" would suck the blood out of their lifeless bodies and then eat the remains. The more commonly used word in the Muscogee language for panther or lion is Katcv (Kat-chuh) according to what Micco Blue of the Holatte Grounds shared with me. The odds of so many cultures worldwide telling the same stories with the same details are beyond chance. In the Native American stories of these giants there are several recurring themes. These are a few of them:

- Most of the giant tribes were red-haired.
- The giants were sexually and ritually sadistic.
- The giants were cannibalistic, frequently raiding nearby Native villages for meals and blood- drinking sacrifices.
- They were seven feet and taller.
- They had six fingers on each hand and six toes on each foot.
- Some stories tell of the giants having double rows of teeth.

Whenever these skeletal remains were found, excavated, or accidentally unearthed they were often sent to the Smithsonian Institute, never to be seen again. Not only do these remains found throughout the country validate the Biblical record, it is also authenticates the oral history of Native American tribes. Unfortunately, the scientific community does not accept indigenous oral history as a valid source of information. Is it strange to think that the fallen angels were once cherubs and seraphs? Of course not. The cherubs had four winged arms and the seraphs had six winged arms. Kokopelli has four protrusions sticking out of his back with another two for playing his flute. Could it be possible that this star person was a fallen seraph?

One day I was in a bookstore when I felt the prompting to pick up a book on tattoo designs. I didn't know why Creator would have me look through a tattoo book, but I picked it up and started flipping through it. The art was page after page of typical tattoo montages of skulls, snakes, hearts, and other designs until I came to a page depicting a Hindu god and goddess. I stood there as illumination at what I was seeing hit me in waves. One of the so-called gods had four arms and the other had six arms! I read the legends of these two demons and sure enough they both "fell from the heavens" and were worshipped as gods. This was a fallen cherub and a fallen seraph taking on the persona of a god/goddess in a country half a world away from here with the same story as what has been told amongst Native people of the Americas.

I received more insight when I read the Book of Enoch. While it is not part of the canonized Bible, it is quoted in the New Testament just like the Book of Jasher. Most see them as history books that fill in some of the background details found in the Old Testament.

If you feel led to read these books just keep in mind that they are not Scripture but they do offer us historical insights. I suggest, if you have an interest in these books, praying and asking the Lord whether or not you should read them. If you read them, I suggest approaching them as reading a history book written by an unverified source. They do not claim to be from the mouth of God, and it is important that we remember that.

That being said, the Book of Enoch goes into detail about the fallen angels and the things they taught mankind, as well many other things that the church deemed heresy at the time such as the earth revolving around the sun. After being cleared by the Lord to read the Book of Enoch one day, I began. What I found shocked me. The name of one of the fallen angels, as transcribe by Enoch who was Noah's great, great grandfather, is Kokabel.

Is this striking resemblance to the name "Kokopelli" merely a coincidence? I don't believe this is any accident of phonetics. Even more disturbing is the breakdown of this false god's name. Koko in the native Zuni language means "Lord or God" and Pelli means "Flies." We find this exact same definition written in Hebrew in the Bible.

Spoken by Achazyah (Ahaziah), *"Go and consult Baal-Zebub, the god of Ekron, to see if I will recover from this injury."* (YHVH -Stern, 1998, p. 2 Kings 1:2)

"And the scribes who came down from Jerusalem were saying, 'He is possessed by Baalzebub', and 'by the prince of demons he casts out the demons.'" (YHVH, 2011, p. Mark 3:22)

Baalzebub was a Philistine god worshipped during Biblical times in the city of Ekron and beyond. In the Hebrew language Ba'al means "Lord" and Zebub means "flies." Based upon this research, if Baalzebub means "Lord of the Flies" and Kokopelli also means "Lord of the Flies," what else is one to conclude other than Baalzebub and Kokopelli are one and the same?

Should I really have been surprised? There is so much waiting to be found in the oral history of Native people that reinforces the Biblical stories and accounts. Years before reading the Book of Enoch, we had rid our home of all things Kokopelli. We realized through the powerful conviction of the Holy Spirit that we had images of a false god decorating our home! This false god had a reputation for raping young girls and taking advantage of women! I wanted no part of him. He along with his image was kicked out of our home and any effigies that we had were destroyed by fire, in accordance with Scriptures:

"You shall put no other gods before me." Exodus 20:3

"The images of their gods you are to burn in the fire." Deuteronomy 7:25

"I am the LORD; that is my name! I will not yield my glory to another or my praise to idols." Isaiah 42:8

Do we dare anger God because of an emotional attachment to a deceptive idol? Since then, I have told many people about the ugly truth of Kokopelli. Some of them are horrified at the intrusion upon their spiritual sanctity.

Others tenaciously cling to their idol saying, "That's not what it means to me." My response: "But what does it mean to your Creator?"

"Now therefore fear the LORD, and serve Him in sincerity and in truth; and put away the gods which your fathers served beyond the River, and in Egypt; and serve ye the LORD. But if serving the LORD seems undesirable to you, then choose for yourselves this day whom you will serve, whether the gods your ancestors served beyond the Euphrates, or the gods of the Amorites, in whose land you are living. But as for me and my household, we will serve LORD." Joshua 24:14-15

Chapter IV: Bridges of Compassion

Joshua came to a crossroad in his life where he had to make a decision that would change his future and his descendants' future forever. Making an absolute stance against idolatry, Joshua later would obediently walk in the perfect timing of God which took down the walls at Jericho. Although this seems so long ago in God's timing, this is a very recent memory to The Creator.

"But do not let this one fact escape your notice, beloved, that with the Lord one day is like a thousand years, and a thousand years like one day." (YHVH, 2011, p. 2 Peter 3:8)

This verse teaches us that time is not seem the same to the Lord. If a day is as a thousand years to Him, then the flood only happened six days ago, and Joshua's promise about his house serving The Lord was made even more recently. The time of the giants and the evil of mankind that brought on the flood doesn't seem as far away when we try to see it through God's reckoning of time. The birth, death, and resurrection of Yeshua (Jesus) was the day before yesterday when you think about it this way. The same is true with the atrocities of Indian massacres and removals which occurred a mere couple of hours ago in the

Lord's estimation of time. It is still a fresh topic to Him and for those who carry generations of pain and difficulty, it is still fresh for them.

Try to think of a time in your life when you have been hurt by someone. Perhaps this person didn't even realize that they hurt you. If the situation was never dealt with, the negative feelings still remain. Without the Biblically-prescribed approach to remedying this hurt, there is no healing and no closure. If the pain is significant enough, you can actually find yourself disliking the person's other family members, even if they had nothing to do with the original offense. If it was a racially-motivated wrong, or if it multiple offenses occur from people all of the same ethnicity, then racial prejudices can ensue and carry on an on for an unlimited amount of time.

This pain and prejudice is what most Native people have received as their birthright. It is an inheritance of offense. Giving up that carefully guarded victim's legacy is difficult. Sometimes other Natives view you as less Native, as less of a warrior, as one who no longer identifies with his people and their history.

In the bartering system we have used since ancient times, we have a saying: "Good trade." When two parties have agreed upon a trade of items, at the end, both parties say, "Good trade." This is their verbal form of signing on the dotted line, and it denotes their satisfaction at how the trade ended.

What many people do not see is that I have traded despair for hope, anger for peace, hatred for love. I have traded an inheritance of offense for a legacy of personal forgiveness of my wrongdoings and that this is what enables me to have an intimate relationship with the Most High God. So, I can enthusiastically say, "Good trade!"

One of the worst things anyone can say to a Native person today is that all of the atrocities are in the past and they should "Get over it." Perhaps people who say that do not understand how difficult it is to "get over it" when there has been no resolution, no righting of the wrongs . . . no justice for Native peoples. When there is no justice, forgiveness and healing are more difficult. When there is no justice, forgiveness and healing are more difficult.

How do we address this issue as believers? Should we sidestep this responsibility of repentance or should we stand in the gap? Knowing that this is a fresh issue in the vast scope of eternity's grandfather clock, I hear this clock chiming that the hour is here for repentance.

What if your ancestors did not perpetrate these acts against Native people? What if they were indigenous supporters, recent immigrants or other indigenous people as well? Repentance on behalf of others is a Biblical concept! We simply cannot step to the side and say, well that was them, or we had nothing to do with it, or my family migrated here long after all of that happened.

I am a patriot through and through, but I also understand that our country was founded on rebellion and bloodshed with hundreds of thousands of heroic lives lost in the pursuit of freedom. This freedom has been redefined over the past 500 years and as we see increased violence, natural disasters, droughts, fires, and more it is obvious in a "post Christian" America (which is what we have been labeled), the Lord's hand of blessing and grace could at any moment, be removed, if indeed it has not been already. In order to turn this tide of indifference a national call of repentance is needed, and a formal heartfelt rending-of-garments-apology from the President of the United States (whoever he or she may be at the time) is needed for these old wounds to heal and for restoration to begin.

Jeremiah 22:3 "This is what Adonai says: "Do what is right and just; rescue the wronged from their oppressors; do nothing wrong or violent to the stranger, orphan or widow; don't shed innocent blood in this place." (YHVH -Stern, 1998)

The root of many of the broken treaties was the lust for gold or other natural resources which were not being used by the tribes who lived on their ancient lands. Over 300 treaties were made between the US Government and various Native American tribes. None of those covenant promises were kept by the United States. Our money says "In God We Trust." Thankfully, it does not say "In

Government We Trust"! There is a common saying among Native Americans that you can often see on bumpers stickers on reservations "Sure you can trust the Government. Ask an Indian."

The God of Abraham, Isaac, and Jacob is a God of Covenant who has never broken His promises. According to Scripture, there are consequences to breaking a treaty (covenant). Here are the Biblical consequences of breaking covenant and not obeying God's commands:

1) Sickness and death - Consumption, fever, tumors, incurable boils (shingles/herpes/pox) and itch, mental illness and death. Deuteronomy 28:15,21-22,27,35,60

a) 1 Corinthians 11:20-39 is a section of Scripture dealing with the taking of what is commonly called communion. This sacrament is a reenactment of the covenant meal of Pesach (Passover).It can be given as an example because it is a covenant meal and one of God's Appointed Times with consequences for disobedience. America has broken covenant not only with First Nations people but also with God and we are still partaking of this covenant meal with these broken treaties unresolved.

Many Believers have chosen to compartmentalize God into an easygoing, Santa-looking jolly man sporting bunny slippers and a "Grace, Peace & Love" t-shirt. It seems commonplace to allow Him to forgive whatever sins we commit without so much as a repentance, to have Him bail us out of the trouble we create, and to forget He is supposed to be our Lord and we, His willing servants. It is easy to leave Him out of the kitchen in matters of healthful living, the bedroom in matters of relationship and intimacy, the voting box in matters of politics, the cubicle in matters of business. Yet in every instance of our lives, He always knows best and always has our own best interests in mind

"But let a man examine himself, and so let him eat of the bread, and let him drink of the cup; for he eating and drinking unworthily eats and drinks judgment to himself. For this reason many among you are weak and feeble, and many are dead." (YHVH, 2011, p. 1 Corinthians 11:28)

Alcohol (Consumption) in America:
Percent of adults 18 years of age and over who were current regular drinkers: 51.5%
Number of alcoholic liver disease deaths: 15,990
Number of alcohol-induced deaths, excluding accidents and homicides: 25,692 (CDC, Centers for Diseas Control and Prevention, 2011)

Cancer in America:
1,638,910 people died of cancer in 2012 (Society, 2012)

Herpes in America (boils and itch):
CDC estimates that, annually, 776,000 people in the United States get new herpes infections. Genital herpes

infection is common in the United States. Nationwide, 16%, or about one out of six, people aged 14 to 49 years have genital HSV-2 infection. (CDC, Center for Diseas Control, September) This statistic is actually suspected to be much higher in unreported populations.

Mental illness in America:
61.5 million Americans experience mental illness in a given year. (Duckworth, 2013)

2) Natural Disaster - Drought, famine, and plagues. We find these disasters throughout Scripture as punishment on the land because of disobedience on man's part. Deuteronomy 22:15,22,24,38,40,42

    a) 2 Chronicles 7:14 *"If my people, who are called by my name, will humble themselves and pray and seek my face and turn from their wicked ways, then I will hear from heaven, and I will forgive their sin and will heal their land."*

These words were spoken by the Lord to King Solomon on the day known as Simchat Torah (translated "Rejoice in the Law"), immediately after the dedication of the temple while celebrating Sukkot which is also known as the Feast of Tabernacles. One of the important aspects of this celebration is praying for God to provide rain.

b) Natural disasters in the United States have increased by over 400% since the 1900's (Guha-Sapir, 2010).

c) It is interesting to note that these numbers are since the forced removal of the Cherokee, Muscogee Creek, Seminole, Chickasaw, and Choctaw people on the Trail of Tears.

3) Defeat- *The Lord is not only our provider but He is also the one who protects us. When we break covenant, He removes His hand of protection and we become vulnerable to attack from our enemies. Then we become objects of scorn and mockery to the nations and subject God to mockery by people who are watching to see how things fare with people in covenant with God.* Deuteronomy 28:25,32-33,44

a) With the moral decline and rampant deterioration of traditional American values that was ushered in during the 1960's, America saw its first national loss in Vietnam. Just because history wants to call it a "conflict" rather than a war is an absurd way to cover over defeat. As a veteran, it seems to me to be an affront to the sacrifice made by American soldiers when they paid the ultimate price: their lives. Ask a veteran who was there and they will tell you: It was war. To all of you reading this right now: Welcome

Home, thank you for your service and your sacrifice for your country. Some carry these scars on the outside and others carry them on the inside. May Creator give you peace in the name of the Yeshua Prince of Peace.

b)   Since September 11th, the sentiment of the global community toward America has been on the decline. It may have even begun before that. We have become the laughing stock of our enemies. No longer do we have the respect, honor or admiration that we once had. It is no "coincidence" that the attack on our soil on that day occurred, according to some Hebraic calendar reckonings, on one of God's Appointed Times called the Feast of Trumpets (Leviticus 23), a day of waking up and repenting.

c)   I am concerned that the time for America winning wars is over unless there is a national repentance and a strong, official and practical stance of supporting the nation of Israel, the apple of God's eye and our only Middle East ally.

4)   The Sojourner - We have also forsaken God's commands in taking care of the immigrants or the sojourners among us. Today, the media gives us the image of immigrants as being migrant workers from Mexico, Central and South American. Roughly 80% of the populations of Mexico are native Indian. Before there were national

borders, this land was all Indian country. Occupants traveled the ancient trade routes of their ancestors throughout the Americas, trading goods, knowledge, and plant seeds. The most recent American census gives us a startling statistic. Mexican Indians are the fourth largest tribal group in the United States of America. (ICTMN, 2013)

The current popular American opinion on immigration is reprehensible to me. Sometimes, one may need to be reminded: Unless every one of your family's ancestors is Native American, some of your ancestors were also immigrants to this country. They were immigrants who came here looking for opportunity and a better life. Yet the sentiment we see today has the descendants of those immigrants closing the borders on those who want the same things their immigrant ancestors from Europe wanted when they came to these lands. There are two ways to address this issue in a manner that is correct in The Lord's eyes. One is a world view and the other is a Godly view. I prefer the Godly view which has never failed despite our own worst errors. What does God have to say about this issue? Here are just a few verses:

a)   Leviticus 19:33-34 *"If a foreigner stays with you in your land, do not do him wrong. Rather, treat the foreigner staying with you like the native-born among you — you are to love him as yourself, for you were foreigners in the land of Egypt; I am Adonai your God."*

b) Exodus 22:20 *"You must neither wrong nor oppress a foreigner living among you,"*

c) Deuteronomy 27:19 *"A curse on anyone who interferes with justice for the foreigner,"*

d) Matthew 5:46-47 *"What reward do you get if you love only those who love you? Why, even tax-collectors do that! And if you are friendly only to your friends, are you doing anything out of the ordinary? Even the Goyim (Gentiles) do that!"*

e) Mathew 25:35-36 *"For I was hungry, and you gave Me something to eat; I was thirsty, and you gave Me something to drink; I was a stranger, and you invited Me in; naked, and you clothed Me; I was sick, and you visited Me; I was in prison, and you came to Me."*

The mission field is moving to us, America! Our very constitution is the basis for equality that cannot be found in any other country in the world. "We hold these truths to be self-evident; that all men are created equal, that they are endowed by their Creator with certain unalienable rights, which among these are life, liberty and the pursuit of happiness."

America's founders knew that inalienable rights of life, liberty, and the pursuit of happiness were given by The Creator and should be ensured by the government.

In 1811, New York Supreme Court Chief Justice James Kent in People v. Ruggles held: "'...whatever strikes at the root of the Bible tends manifestly to the dissolution of civil government....' We are a Christian people, and the morality of the country is deeply engrafted upon the Bible.... The Bible in its enlarged sense, as a religion revealed and taught in the Bible, is part and parcel of the law of the land..." (People v. Ruggles, 1811)

The South Carolina Supreme Court upheld the Christian foundation of this nation when it ruled in 1844 " Charleston v. Benjamin, - "The Bible is part of the common law of the land, with liberty of conscience to all. It has always been so recognized.... Judge Nathaniel Freeman in 1802 charged Massachusetts Grand Juries as follows: "The laws of the Christian system, as embraced by the Bible, must be respected as of high authority in all our courts.... [Our government] originating in the voluntary compact of a people who in that very instrument profess the Christian religion, it may be considered, not as republic Rome was a Pagan, but a Christian republic." (City of Charleston v Benjamin, 1846)

With each case that the government upheld the law by definition of its Christian foundation, it reaffirmed its covenant promises with God. While man has taken covenant lightly throughout the centuries, God does not as evidenced throughout Scripture. The Good Book, as they say in the Deep South, shows times of curses brought upon a nation when forsaking covenant and, in fewer situations, blessings of ruling a nation according to His ways.

Scripture does tell us to abide by the laws of the land. There is a way to immigrate into America which is legal and honoring to God by doing it in accordance with the law. However, how can you tell at a glance who is here legally or not? Is that up to you to pass judgment, or are we to set the example by treating one another as human beings first? Is it not bad enough that from the comfort of our own homes, we turn a blind eye to the inhumane treatment and violence that befalls the citizens of other nations? How can we fault these victims who come to this country for a better life? As believers hoping to please the Lord, we cannot continue to ignore the plight of the sojourners among us who merely want the same things that most Europeans wanted when they came centuries ago.

We belong to the Kingdom of Heaven, an eternal kingdom. Therefore, we should think and act as our King thinks and acts. . How did Yeshua (Jesus) The Messiah treat sojourners in His land? We are all called to a ministry of reconciliation no matter where you are living or where you are from. If you are a Native American believer, then this opportunity of hospitality falls upon you even more as an instrument of peace between nations and racial reconciliation between people. The time is now for this healing work as God has been placing the microphone to mouths of First Nations people so that our voices can be heard throughout the nations of the world. The first step to take is the most important to prepare our hearts.

First, is to repent from all of our wrongdoing. To repent means not just to say we are sorry for something, but to do our best to cease doing it. Its stopping in your tracks and doing a 180 degree turn without looking back. Next, accept Creator's gift to you: The forgiveness that comes with embracing His Son, Yeshua, who laid down His life in payment for all of our wrongdoings. He is our Kippur, or covering for atonement so that we could live not just a life of closeness with The Creator but also an eternal life of closeness with Him after this one is finished.

Ask for Creator's Holy Spirit to fill you. Listen for His voice, as He is your true and new Holy Spirit guide, directing and teaching you on this ancient path. Then ask for divine love. This is a prayer that God is waiting to answer. He wants us to love above all else. Love is the very essence of God. His Son was love embodied. We are to be the same: instruments of love, played by our Heavenly Father for all to hear and enjoy.

"The person who doesn't love does not know God, because God is love." (YHVH, 2011, p. 1 John 4:8)

After that, tell Creator that you are only human and do not know how to forgive, but you are willing to learn. Forgiveness is not a feeling or an emotion. Forgiveness is a decision. Sometimes it comes easier than others. Sometimes the work of forgiveness is completed instantly. Other times, it takes many years and tears to be complete. Now that you have been given some measure of love from God as a gift, forgiveness will be easier than it was before love was amplified in you. Forgiveness, even toward other people, is vital to our relationship with Creator.

"For if you forgive others their offenses, your heavenly Father will also forgive you; 15 but if you do not forgive others their offenses, your heavenly Father will not forgive yours." (YHVH -Stern, 1998, pp. Matthew 6:14-15)

It is hard to understand how forgiving a wrong can help us heal from its effects. Perhaps it is something that we are not meant to comprehend. When I was broken in true repentance and I cried out to be delivered from the hate I had for the Spaniards for what they did to my people, God answered me! I decided that I would not continue in the bondage of hate over a fellow human being for what their ancestors had done to mine. God took my hate away and filled it with His love when I was willing to break my own heart of stone.

Psalm 34:18 *"The LORD is close to the brokenhearted and saves those who are crushed in spirit."* (YHVH, 2011)

Chapter V: Resolving to Reconcile

I kept finding that many of the Holy Men and Women from different tribes were what I call "closet believers." They walked in the traditional ways. To fully do so was to believe the stories that had been passed down through the generations. They also knew the stories had to stay alive and had to continue as tradition dictates.

These stories are a small key to the awakening of many First Nations tribes who sorely need intercessory prayer. If you feel that call from the Holy Spirit to stand in the gap as an intercessor, peacemaker, or bridge builder be obedient to your calling but get prepared first. I would personally suggest the following books about First Nations people and bringing the Gospel in a good way that won't be perceived as harmful to the culture.

One Church Many Tribes by Richard Twiss, Warfare by Honor by Qaumaniq and Suuqiina, and Introduction to First Nations Ministry by Cheryl Bear are a great place to begin your learning. Above all, allow His Holy Spirit to lead you in everything when heeding the call to native ministry. Time is short, and the workers are few who are willing to warrior up as intercessors in the spirit world. Don't be afraid to speak out on behalf of the Lord's heart for Native people; you might be surprised at what happens.

When we were on the road ministering and teaching throughout the country, Laralyn and I were asked to speak at a traditional Baptist Church in Columbus, Georgia. The Lord had given us a word to speak concerning reconciliation and forgiveness, and so we prepared the prior evening to give this message that Sunday morning. The church was white and built with the southern charm typical of places of worship built in the early 1900's. After we were introduced by the pastor, we walked up and looked at the sea faces of God's saints sitting in the dark wooden pews.

We were both struck at the stark contrast, literally, of what we were seeing. All the "white" people were on one side of the church and all the "black" people were on the other and here we were, the "red" man and woman in the middle. There was a stifling sensation and spiritual stiffness in the atmosphere that was completely noticeable from the pulpit that we hadn't experienced when we were sitting in the pew.

We told the congregation that we were not going to say another word until everyone stood up and moved to sit next to a family from a color or race other than theirs. Then once they found that other family they were to embrace them and greet them as brothers and sisters at which point we could resume the service.

1 Peter 5:14 *"Greet ye one another with a kiss of love. Peace be with you all who are in Messiah Yeshua. Amen."*

Some of the people looked around nervously which prompted Laralyn to say, "Come on now, we don't have much time, and we aren't starting until you do this." We looked at each one another as the atmosphere began to change in the church and I recalled Yeshua once saying:

Matthew 5:47 *"And if you greet only your own people, what are you doing more than others? Do not even Gentiles do that?"*

We watched as people got up and looked around as if they had never seen the inside of their church before. Then they began to walk towards each other with trepidation but then something incredible happened. The saints began to shake hands, hug, and smile at each other. Laughter and the love of God began to flow among the people in the congregation and it was noticeable on everyone's faces. People were grinning and children were giggling as they got situated, and the whole atmosphere of the church had changed into one of joy, peace, and love.

After the service, the pastor came up to us and said that what had happened was exactly why he had asked us to come to his church. He had tried for years but couldn't get them to do what a couple of Indians bearing flutes, drums, and the love of the Lord had done in one service. All glory to Elohim who breaks down the walls of division and brings us together in unity.

The Lord commands us to love one another, to forgive one another, and to be in unity with each other. To reject His commands is to inadvertently reject Him.

Exodus 20:5 *"…I, the LORD your God, am a jealous God who will not tolerate your affection for any other gods. I lay the sins of the parents upon their children; the entire family is affected--even children in the third and fourth generations of those who reject me."* (YHVH, 2011)

Unfortunately, in the above instance, many of the people rejected the commandment to love one another (along with many others commandments). When truly walking in His love, we won't steal, lie, murder, bear false witness, or commit other sins.

Scholars typically regard a Biblical generation as forty years. That means three or four generations is about 120-160 years. With this calculation, it puts the punishments related to the atrocities committed with the removal of the Five Civilized Tribes from their ancient homelands and many other tribes during this generation as just recently expired.

There is no coincidence that exactly 160 years after the beginning of the forced removals, the movie Dances with Wolves was released to the nation. This movie caused many people to fall to their knees in heart-rending repentance concerning the actions of their forefathers against

First Nations people. We need to be willing to know and see history through the eyes of the First Nations people in order to connect with our hearts and mourns with our brothers and sisters of Turtle Island. This is part of the reconciliation process. Recently the State of Tennessee made a tremendous leap forward in reconciliation when the legislators unanimously passed a resolution expressing regret for its involvement in the Trail of Tears. This is reconciliation at a government level and heartily welcomed! Laralyn and I were deeply moved to have been asked to be a part of this historic day.

The marble walls of the Nashville, Tennessee capitol building sang back the echoes of the Native American dance bells, jingles, drums, and flutes that were being prepared for this historic day. There was a palpable excitement in the air as First Nations' leaders, and elders began to arrive from different tribes as well as others who are descendants of those who walked the Trail of Tears. The capitol staff had meticulously gone through the building taking down every portrait of Andrew Jackson so as to not cause offense with the exception of a few bronze busts too heavy to carry. People's hearts were ready for reconciliation and inner healing to begin while a few felt it was long overdue.

To commemorate the 175th Anniversary of the Trail of Tears, the Tennessee General Assembly unanimously passed House Joint Resolution 553 on Friday June 27th at the State Capitol. According to HR553, the Tennessee General Assembly acknowledges the role played by the Volunteer State that led to Native American homes and lands being confiscated before being rounded up and forcibly removed to Indian Territory, now known as Oklahoma, starting in 1838 and concluding in 1839. The following excerpt is from the resolution.

"The state of Tennessee wishes to both acknowledge this tragedy and renounce any role it may have played in what is a stain on our collective histories," the resolution states. "Tennesseans stand against acts of injustice perpetrated against any people or group regardless of race, gender, or religion. Therefore, we offer our sincere regret to the Cherokee, Chickasaw, Yuchi, Creek, Choctaw, and Shawnee Nations and all Native American nations who were tragically and unjustly confined and removed from their lands by our participation in the Removal Act of 1830 and the subsequent death march known as the Trail of Tears."

Tennessee lawmakers voted across party lines for this resolution to pass when it was presented to them in in 2013. It may seem like a short journey but it actually began eight years ago through the collective efforts of several ministries uniting for a common cause regardless of denominational differences. We would travel often to many of these prayer meetings pleading with God to heal the land and the people through the powerful movement of reconciliation which all believers are called to according to:

2 Corinthians 5:18 *"And it is all from God, who through the Messiah has reconciled us to himself and has given us the ministry of reconciliation,"*

Three mighty women of God, Daphne Swilling, Dr. Bettye Lundquist, and Kim Driver, took the call to heart for being bridge builders of reconciliation and healing between First Nations and the US Government. My wife and I, Laralyn RiverWind, spent several years traveling throughout the Southeastern United States in ministry answering this same call. We were honored when asked to speak and perform our original song "The Trail Where They Cried" by The Blessed Blend- nominated for Best Historical Song by the Native American Music Awards, on the day the resolution was read. This moving song takes the listener on a short journey through some of the trials of the forced removal ending with a message of hope and healing in Yeshua (Jesus) the Messiah.

The Godly roots of our Christian nation were evident in the presentation of this resolution whose goal is to take a holy tomahawk to this 500 year old root of bitterness, prejudice, and greed. When the resolution was read the House Chamber erupted in cheers, the women's lulu's, war cries, shofar blasts, and people joyfully crying. This was a historic first with Tennessee doing something that no other state has done before in acknowledging their role in the Trail of Tears. Every federally recognized tribal leader asked to speak gave powerful statements of healing and sincere thanks for the passing of the resolution. Clifton Petit (Cherokee Nation Oklahoma) ended the proceedings by praying in the Cherokee language and asking God to bless the State of Tennessee for what they had accomplished on this day.

It may seem odd to apologize for something that no one alive today did, but to First Nations' people the memories are still a part of who they are. Some of the people who attended this event grew up hearing their great-grandparents talk about how they survived the forced march. While it may seem like history to the majority of Americans the emotional pain has been carried for several generations by Native Americans. The acknowledgement of what was done was enough for many, but in addition to the resolution, the legislators were truly heartfelt in their speeches of regret for the actions of the State of Tennessee regarding the Native relocation.

One hundred seventy-five years ago, the forced removal was opposed by U.S. Representative Davy Crockett of Tennessee, who made a politically risky but morally righteous objection to Indian Removal. David Crockett was born in 1786 into a loving pioneer family that lived on the Nolichucky River in East Tennessee. He became one of the biggest proponents for Native American rights, openly voicing his disdain for President Andrew Jackson. The incredible story of Davy Crockett actually goes back to when his grandparents immigrated to the United States from Ireland with the whole family and headed out west to settle. Davy's entire family, except for his father John, was killed by a band of Muscogee Creek warriors. Despite this tragic loss in his own family at Native hands, Crockett became the prominent voice in the government decrying the forced removal act.

"It was expected of me that I was to bow to the name of Andrew Jackson, and follow him in all his motions, and windings, and turnings, even at the expense of my con-sciences and judgment. Such a thing was new to me, and a total stranger to my principles. ... His famous, or rather I should say infamous Indian bill was brought forward and, I opposed it from the purest motives in the world. Several of my colleagues got around me, and told me how well they loved me, and that I was ruining myself. They said it was a favorite measure of the President, and I ought to go for it. I told them I believed it was a wicked unjust measure, and that I should go against it, let the cost to myself be what it might; that I was willing to go with General Jackson in everything that I believed was honest and right; but further than this, I wouldn't go for him, or any other man in the whole creation."

Crockett's stance on the removal may have cost him the office of President of the United States. This formerly well-loved representative soon became very isolated by most of the politicians in Tennessee as he continued to voice his rejection of the removal policy. Among his epic remarks on that key debate day, remain two of his well-known quotes to his fellow legislators: "One day you will meet your maker and you will have to answer for what you have done." And the other, "You all can go to hell, I'm going to Texas!" There in the Lone Star State, Davey Crockett life was cut short at the Alamo on March 6th, 1836. (Crockett, 1834)

Our prayer is that more states will follow in the example of government officials of the State of Tennessee and bring another chapter in our collective American history to a close. The State of Georgia sent two delegates to watch the proceedings at the capitol building, and we hope they report what an incredible display of compassion and repentance there was on this historic day. Let the healing begin across our great nation for wrongs in the past so that our future generations can look boldly ahead.

Chapter VI: Morning Song

The song of the cicadas slightly changed to a lower pitch orchestra as the first glimmers of light began to make their way across the darkness. Although the fire had begun to dwindle down to a few embers, the beauty of the sun rising through the forest seemed as if it caused everything to stand still for a moment and acknowledge the beauty of Creator's handiwork. The birds began to warm up their voices for the morning chorus of praising the One who created the sun and caused it to rise once more in the east.

We both walked to the bubbling creek as the morning sun began its ascent into the sky. Slowly, the night retreated into the shadows of itself while we prepared for the morning song and prayer. The crystal clear mountain waters flowed around my feet and ankles as I placed one foot before the other into the running waters, making little clouds of silt rise around them. As the sun continued to rise, we both bent at the knees while we faced the east and slowly filled our hands with the cool mountain waters. Seven times we each poured water over our heads as the sun rose before us. Seven times we lifted our hands to the Creator acknowledging Him to be the one who guides our paths. We began to sing an ancient going-to-water song.

The words are a simple declaration to begin your day, "A Wen-day Yah Ho "which translates into "I Belong to Yah."

It felt as if the birds were singing along with us while the trees clapped their leaves in time to the song. Giving the Creator the first of your day makes all the difference in how things will turn out for you. Slowly turning my head, I looked at my old friend, PipeCarrier, as his eyes moistened and his lip began to slightly quiver. I respectfully looked away and started back to where we had sat all evening. Covering it with dirt to make sure the fire wouldn't blaze up once we left, I stood up and was ready to start walking home. PipeCarrier reached his arm out for me to grasp as is customary to his people.

I received his arm within mine as we clasped forearm to forearm and then embraced one another while speaking blessings over one another. PipeCarrier then looked me deep in the eyes as he clasped my arm and said, "I have prayed and asked Tunkashila for a Lakota name for you." He paused for a slight moment as he looked at the vast forest around us.

"Four days I have prayed and gone without food or water. Creator heard my prayers, and I have been given a name for you to be known by my people." PipeCarrier leaned in close and said, "Mini Wakan" is your name to my people. Mini Wakan means "Sacred Water" in the Lakota language.

I was shocked and honored to receive such a beautiful name. We spoke about the name, Mini Wakan, and what it represents in my life. We finished speaking and began gathering our things for the journey home through the forest. Leisurely, we began to walk down the forest trail in silence. Not only absorbing the beauty of the forest waking up around us but also processing the things we had spoken of throughout the evening.

Little did I know that later in our friendship we would lay hands on PipeCarrier and The Creator would touch his body when he was in need of healing from a life threatening ailment. PipeCarrier accepted Yeshua (Jesus) as his personal Lord and Savior and then received the gift of the Holy Spirit. He is now active among his Lakota people in ministry and spreading the Good News. Who is like You, oh Yah, among the gods? There are none like Him!

"That's What the Old Ones Say..."

Bibliography

Adair, J. (1775). *Out of the Flames.* Cherokee Language & Culture (1998).

Barnes, P. M. (2005). *Vital and Health Statistics- Health Characteristics of the American Indian and Alaska Native Adult Population.* Atlanta: Centers for Disease Control and Prevention.

Baum, L. F. (1890, December 20). The Sitting Bull Editorial. *The Saturday Pioneer,* p. 1.

Baum, L. F. (1891, January 3). The Wounded Knee Editorial. *The Saturday Pioneed,* p. 1.

Casas, B. d. (1552). *A Short Account of the Destruction of the Indies.* New York: Penguin Books.

CDC. (2011, December). *Centers for Diseas Control and Prevention.* Retrieved January 6th, 2014, from Alcohol Abuse-Series 10 Number 256: http://www.cdc.gov/nchs/fastats/alcohol.htm

CDC. (September, 6th 2012). *Center for Diseas Control.* Retrieved January 6th, 2014, from Sexually Transmitted Diseases: http://www.cdc.gov/std/herpes/stdfact-herpes.htm

City of Charleston v Benjamin, 2 Strob. 508 (South Carolina Supreme 1846).

Columbus, C. (1493). *"Introduction to the Letters from America",-Ife, Barry W-1992.* Strand: King's College London.

Crockett, D. (1834). *Narrative of the Life of David Crockett, of the State of Tennessee.* Reprint Services Corporation.

Deacon, R. (1966). *Madoc and the Discovery of America: Some New Light on an Old Controversy.* New York: George Braziller, Inc.

Duckworth, D. K. (2013, March). *National Alliance of Mental Illness.* Retrieved January 6th, 2014, from NAMI: http://www.nami.org/factsheets/mentalillness_factsheet.pdf

Foundation, A. I. (2010). *Pine Ridge Statistics.* Brigham City: American Indian Humanitarian Foundation.

Grantham, B. (2002). *Creation Myths and Legends of the Creek Indians.* Gainesville: University Press of Florida.

Guha-Sapir, P. (2010). *Centre for Research on Epidemiology of Disasters.* Geneva: United Nations International Strategy for Disaster Reduction Secretariat .

Hackett, J. A., & Coogan, M. D. (2001). *The Oxford Guide to People & Places of the Bible.* Oxford: Oxford University Press.

ICTMN. (2013, August 8th). *Indian Country Today Media Network.* Retrieved January 6th, 2014, from Indian Country Today Media Network: http://indiancountrytodaymedianetwork.com/2013/08/05/fourth-largest-tribe-united-states-mexicans-150740

Langer, G. (2012, July 18). *Poll: Most Americans Say They're Christian*. Retrieved July 2, 2014, from ABC News: http://abcnews.go.com/US/story?id=90356

Lewis, C. (1940). *The Problem of Pain*. New York: HarperCollins.

Lossiah, L. K. (1998). *The Secrets and Mysteries of the Cherokee Little People, Yuñwi Tsunsdi'*. Cherokee: Cherokee Publications.

Martin, J. W. (2000). *The Land Looks After Us : A History of Native American Religion: A History*. New York: Oxford University Press.

Murphy, G. (1997, August 1). *Modern History Sourcebook: The Constitution of the Iroquois Confederacy*. Retrieved January 4th, 2014, from Fordham University: http://www.fordham.edu/halsall/mod/iroquois.asp

Neihardt, o. G. (2008). *Black Elk Speaks*. New York: University of New York Press.

Nerburn, K. (2009). *The Wolf at Twilight: An Indian Elder's Journey through a Land of Ghosts and Shadow*. Novato: New World Library.

Payne-Butrik(1830). (2010). *The Payne-Butrick Papers-Indians of the Southeast*. University of Nebraska Press.

People v. Ruggles, 8 Johns. R. 290 (New York Superior 1811).

Report of the Commissioner of Indian Affairs for 1891, v. 1.-1. (1891). *"Lakota Accounts of the Massacre at Wounded Knee"*. PBS.

Rouse, I. (1992). *The Tainos- Rise and Decline of the People Who Greeted Columbus.* New Haven: Yale University Press.

Society, A. C. (2012). *Cancer.org.* Retrieved January 6th, 2014, from American Cancer Society: http://www.cancer.org/acs/groups/content/@epidemiol ogysurveilance/documents/document/acspc-031941.pdf

Starr, E. (1984). *History of the Cherokee Indians .* Muskogee, Oklahoma: HOFFMEAN PRINTING CO., INC. .

Suuqiina, D. (2008, 1 10). Indigenous Messengers International. (J. RiverWind, Interviewer)

Thomas, R. K. (1953). *"The Origin and Development of the Redbird Smith Movement".* University of Arizona.

YHVH. (2011). *Common English Bible (CEB).* Nashville: Church Publishing Inc.

YHVH -Stern, D. H. (1998). *Complete Jewish Bible.* Clarksville: Jewish New Testament Publications, INC.

Dedication

I dedicate my first fruit of my literary work to my Heavenly Father and my Messiah and Savior Yeshua. My hope is that what I teach and write is pleasing to The Creator and healing to the nations. To my loving wife, Laralyn, who has spent many evenings without me as I was glued to the computer writing and researching in order that I could complete this book. To all of my brothers and sisters in The Lord whose words of encouragement helped motivate me every day. I also dedicate this book to the Body of Messiah in hopes that more First Nations people will be set free and healed from the past as they step into a deeper relationship with The Creator, experience the transforming power of the Holy Spirit and accept the gift of eternal life through Chief CornerStone Yeshua, His only begotten Son.

About the Author

Chief Joseph RiverWind is an ordained minister along with his wife, soon to be Naturopathic Dr. Laralyn RiverWind. Their home congregation is Beth Yeshua International in Macon, Ga. He is a US Army  Veteran and a nationally acclaimed Native American Music Award (NAMMY) winning musician. He holds a Bachelor in Social Sciences from Mercer University as well as a Masters in Biblical Studies. They have tirelessly educated the public concerning Native American issues, history, spirituality, culture and the arts from kindergarten children to military generals for almost two decades.

The RiverWinds teachings specialize in biblical history, the Feasts of the Lord, Native American contextuality in the church, cultural expressions of worship, Hebraic roots of the faith as well as building bridges of unity, forgiveness and reconciliation. They have both spoken and sung at events such as the 2013 Presidential Inaugural Prayer Breakfast and countless other ministry conferences, entrepreneurial, military, and First Nations events.

website: TheOldOnesSay.com

email: contact@TheOldOnesSay.com

Address:

PO Box 1408

Murphy, NC 28906

The Author's Music CD Releases

Journeys through the Mist
Nominated for 4 NAMMAs

Inspirational Eclectic Fusion

An Interesting blend of contemporary, folk & traditional sounds on original & ancient songs.

Whispers of the Trees
Best-Selling Instrumental

Harp, Native Flute, Nature

For prayer, relaxation, stress relief, spa day and meditating on Creator's word.

Tribal Thunder
Best Rock Recording, 2011

Native American Music Awards

Intense songs. Upbeat drums, sweet Native flute, ethereal vocals, occasional bagpipes and a few more surprises that will get you up and dancing.

Next CD
Contact us if you would like to help fund a future CD. We have many songs waiting for studio time.

You can email Chief Joseph RiverWind with your questions and comments at jriverwind@wordbranch.com.

If you liked That's What the Old Ones Say, please leave feedback.

We recommend other fine Word Branch Publishing Books:

The Morning Road to Thanksgiving by Larry Spotted Crow Mann: http://www.wordbranch.com/the-mourning-road-to-thanksgiving.html

4-Ever-in-My Heart by Terrie McClay: http://www.wordbranch.com/4-ever-in-my-heart.html

Scattered Leaves-The Legend of Ghostkiller by Lynnie Prince: http://www.wordbranch.com/scattered-leaves.html